The Poor and Their Money

Praise for *The Poor and Their Money*

'I found this book extremely stimulating and thought pro-
voking. It also helps outline strategies for financial sector
reforms which seek to empower the poor'
Manmohan Singh, Prime Minister of India

'Rutherford demonstrates not only the reasons why poor
people need financial services ... but also, importantly for
donors, how we can learn from them.'
*Clare Short, former Secretary of State, Department for Interna-
tional Development, UK.*

If you have time to read just one book on microfinance,
make it this one. If you have time for two, read this one
twice. Rutherford offers fresh perspectives, draws surprising
connections, and floats ideas that transform how we think
about poverty.
*Jonathan Morduch, Professor of Public Policy and Economics at
New York University and Managing Director of the Financial
Access Initiative*

'One of the best things we've ever read on microfinance'
CGAP

'This is a small book with a large punch, a punch that KOs
the myth that poor people don't save. If you want to work
in microfinance you should first read this book; it will surely change your notion of how poor people deal with life.'
Dale Adams, Professor Emeritus, The Ohio State University.

The Poor and Their Money

Microfinance from a twenty-first century consumer's perspective

Stuart Rutherford
with Sukhwinder Arora

PRACTICAL ACTION
Publishing

Practical Action Publishing Ltd
Schumacher Centre for Technology and Development
Bourton on Dunsmore, Rugby,
Warwickshire CV23 9QZ, UK
www.practicalactionpublishing.org

© Practical Action Publishing Ltd, 2009

First edition published by Oxford University Press, 2000

ISBN 978 1 85339 688 5

A catalogue record for this book is available from the British
Library.

The authors have asserted his/her rights under the Copyright
Designs and Patents Act 1988 to be identified as authors of this
work.

Since 1974, Practical Action Publishing (formerly Intermediate
Technology Publications and ITDG Publishing) has published
and disseminated books and information in support of
international development work throughout the world.
Practical Action Publishing Ltd (Company Reg. No. 1159018)
is the wholly owned publishing company of Practical Action
Ltd. Practical Action Publishing trades only in support of its
parent charity objectives and any profits are covenanted back
to Practical Action (Charity Reg. No. 247257, Group VAT
Registration No. 880 9924 76).

The first edition of this book, and the research upon it was
based, were supported by funding from the Department for
International Development, UK.

Typeset by S.J.I. Services
Printed and bound in Great Britain by
CPI Antony Rowe, Chippenham and Eastbourne

Front cover photo credit: Curt Carnemark/The World Bank

Contents

Figures

Tables

Foreword

Elizabeth Littlefield
Chief Executive Officer, CGAP

When it was first published in 2000, this jewel of a book introduced readers to the surprisingly sophisticated ways in which poor people manage their money. *The Poor and Their Money* gave us compelling insights into the ways that poor people use financial services, with or without access to formal financial institutions. Its refreshing style and human perspective made it an instant 'classic', read by students of microfinance the world over.

This new edition of the book retains Stuart's trademark clarity and style, while incorporating new learning and insights. By putting poor people's needs at the centre of the story, it offers a superb introduction for the general reader, as well being a rich guide for microfinance experts.

What Stuart captured so brilliantly in his original essay was the simple idea of how savings and borrowing are two sides of the same coin – the yin and the yang of financial services. He explains that both savers and borrowers are simply transforming small amounts of available cash into useful lump sums of money, whether that useful lump sum comes at the beginning and then is paid off in increments (borrowing), or it comes at the end, having been accumulated over time (saving up). The aim of financial systems, he shows us, is to safely and conveniently smooth the flow of money between borrowers and savers.

In recent years microfinance has attracted intense interest from investment funds and Wall Street. The supply of cross border financing has contributed to a growth spurt in microfinance. Amid all the attention to investor appetite and new foreign investment funds, the importance of savings, both as a critical service for poor people and as a funding source, has been in the shadows. Stuart's work helps us balance this supply side focus with the demand side – the needs of poor clients.

That realization of the essential role of savings in poor people's financial lives shifts the whole perspective of microfinance, historically so driven by micro*credit*. It leads to a vision of financial markets that can serve the full range of poor people's needs – collecting and safely holding deposits, prudently lending to bridge cash flow gaps, insuring risks, and moving money around a country or across borders safely and efficiently.

Poor people find ways to save, both formal and informal. When they have safe, convenient, and liquid savings services available, more prefer to save than to borrow – they know saving is both a cheaper and a less risky way for them to accumulate a useful lump sum of money.

Most households are net savers. Most countries are net savers. When microfinance institutions become licensed to mobilize deposits, they gain more depositors than borrowers. The ratio of savers to borrowers is about 10-to-1 for Bank Rakyat Indonesia, 9-to-1 for Centenary Bank in Uganda, and 4-to-1 for PRODEM in Bolivia.

In Africa, microfinance institutions that can mobilize deposits cover 90 per cent of their assets with deposits. In Latin America that number is 65 per cent. But poor peoples' propensity to save is often overlooked, as it is largely informal.

The Poor and Their Money has played a central role in focusing attention on poor people's real behaviour and needs – especially the need for safe, liquid savings – rather than just on the services that their suppliers are used to delivering.

Updating the story of microfinance, this new edition of the book uses findings from the financial diaries projects to reinforce Stuart's earlier work on what poor people look for – deposit and transfer services for day-to-day money management, ways to save bigger sums over the longer haul, and loans for all kinds of needs (not just microenterprise).

If the goal of microfinance is amelioration of poverty, empowerment of women, and other kinds of social development, we will achieve it only by creating vibrant local financial markets that respond to the real wants and needs of poor people. *The Poor and Their Money* helps us keep the clients at the centre of our work.

World Bank,
Washington DC
October 2008

Preface to the Second Edition

This book is about how poor people in developing countries manage their money. It describes how they handle their savings, from keeping bank notes under the floorboards to running sophisticated savings and loan clubs. It illustrates the variety of moneylenders and deposit collectors who serve them, including the new microfinance organizations (MFOs) whose rise has been so spectacular over the last 30 years.

The book explains why poor people who have so little money have such a voracious appetite for good ways to manage it, and illustrates the principles that underlie the devices and services that work best for them. In short, the book is about how a better *understanding* of financial services for the poor can lead to better *provision* of such services.

The audience we have in mind includes not just those who provide or promote or support financial services for the poor by working in MFOs, banks, co-operatives, governments, aid agencies, and research institutions, but also students and members of the general public with an interest in economics or development or the fight against poverty.

The book therefore aims at clarity. We try to avoid jargon. The pages are not cluttered with abbreviations or footnotes. Notes provide some background and a little gossip, and point to further reading.

Nearly all the cases that are used to illustrate our points are ones that the main author has investigated for himself during more than 30 years of research and practice in the subject on three continents. There is a fairly strong bias towards Asia, where the two authors worked together collecting evidence for our ideas. Our main source, then, has been many years of conversations with poor people about how they actually use financial services, and we have not made any statements that are not based on this kind of experience. Sometimes those conversations took place as part of carefully planned research studies, such as the 'financial diaries' projects reported in Chapter Six, while at other times they were held when good luck enabled us to encounter interesting people and to hear their stories during less structured trips to the villages and slums.

The book is not a manual. We do not provide guidance on how to set up an MFO. Although in Chapter Two, we describe the MFO *Safe*Save, set up by the main author in the slums of Dhaka in 1996, we do not mean to imply that *Safe*Save is the last word in financial services for the poor. It is included to illustrate some important points, not as a recommended 'recipe' for microfinance. Because the book's main actors are the users of services, rather than the suppliers, we do not aim to tell the full history of microfinance, which is now long and complex. In Chapter Five, where we discuss microfinance organizations, we make no attempt to mention all the sector's many achievements worldwide. Instead, we focus on a handful of internationally important examples that we happen to know very well, and which illustrate particularly important advances. Grameen Bank and ASA feature, for example, because the main author studied Grameen carefully for three years from 2002 to 2005, and was on the Board of ASA in the late 1990s. Similarly, Sukhwinder Arora has recently studied three rapidly growing MFIs, and through his association with the NGOs ActionAid and CARE International, and with SIDBI (Small Industries Development Bank of India), has worked intensively with the microfinance sector in India.

A version of Chapters One and Two circulated on the internet from early 1998, and was published in February 1999 by the Finance and Development Research Programme of the Institute for Development Policy and Management (IDPM) at the University of Manchester (UK) as 'The Poor and Their Money', *Working Paper Number 3*.

The first edition of the full book was published in 2000 with support from the Department for International Development (DFID, official British aid) and from CGAP, a club of microfinance donors and supporters based at the World Bank in Washington.

This second edition preserves the same general structure as the first. The main themes of the book are timeless, so the first four chapters, where we explore those themes, are not greatly changed from the first edition, except, we hope, in the elimination of some errors. The fifth chapter has been extensively updated to include developments in the microfinance movement in the first decade of the twenty-first century. The final chapter has been recast entirely in a way that reflects the maturing of microfinance: some of the suggestions made to microfinance suppliers in the earlier edition have now become redundant because they have been fully absorbed into the industry. The chapter also describes some research done by the main author since the first edition came out.

In the first edition we wrote that 'the microfinance industry is in its adolescence. There have been encouraging breakthroughs... but the potential for growth and improvement is huge. There are still millions of poor people to reach, and hundreds of new ways of reaching them waiting to be discovered and developed.'

Looking back from 2009, we can see that some of the growth potential has been realized, and prospects are good for the momentum to continue. But each new advance opens up new avenues to explore; new ways to help poor people make sure that their small incomes do not deprive them of safe and profitable ways of managing their money. We hope that our book will further accelerate this voyage of discovery.

Stuart Rutherford and Sukhwinder Arora,
Nagoya and Oxford,
February 2009

Acknowledgements

I was persuaded to write the first edition of this book by Sukhwinder Arora, at that time working for the UK Government's 'Department for International Development' (DFID) in Delhi. Some of the material I use was uncovered in Sukhwinder's company in South Asian cities and villages in the course of work for DFID. He is owed a triple vote of thanks: for encouraging the original edition, for helping to research the material, and for joining me in preparing this new edition. Special thanks also to Elizabeth Littlefield for writing the new Foreword. Graham Wright, now heading *MicroSave*, an organization working to improve microfinance, is another co-researcher who encouraged me, and who tramped through villages and slums with me in Bangladesh, The Philippines, and East Africa. Other colleagues who have been directly involved with me in researching material used in the book include David Hulme, Imran Matin, Md Maniruzzaman, and my assistant S. K. Sinha. I have enjoyed many hours of discussion and debate with Mark Staehle, who more than anyone else helped turn *Safe-Save* from a hobbyist's experiment into a proper functioning MFO.

Further help and encouragement has come from many other sources. They include the organizations for whom or with whom I have worked. Although there are too many to list, I would like to pick out ASA, ActionAid (especially in Bangladesh and Vietnam), BRAC, BURO Tangail, CARE International, CGAP, DFID, Grameen Bank, and PLAN International, as well as my own MFO *Safe*Save and my own academic institutions, the Institute for Development Policy and Management (IDPM) and the Brooks World Poverty Institute, both at the University of Manchester. Fellow instructors and students at the Boulder Microfinance Training Course and at the Southern New Hampshire Microenterprise and Development Institute greatly helped to refine the presentation of the ideas. The many others who have helped through discussion or through reading drafts of this essay (or parts of it) include Edward Abbey, Dale Adams, Dewan Alamgir, Hugh Allen, Alison Barrett, Thierry Van Bastelaer, Ted Baumann, John Burton, Greg Chen, Bob Christen, Robert Christie, Daryl Collins, David Cracknell, Rick Davies, Asif Dowla, Tom Easton, Prabhu Ghate, Hege Gulli, Malcolm Harper, Syed Hashemi, Emrul Hassan, Brigit Helms, Robert Hickson, Madeline Hirschland, Feisal Hussain, Sanae Ito, Henry Jackelen, Susan Johnson, Margaret Kirton, Bill Maddocks, Vijay Mahajan, Elizabeth McCall, Mohini Malhotra, Brett Matthews, Richard Meyer, Richard Montgomery, Karen Moore, Jonathan Morduch, Harry Mugwanga, Leonard Mutesasera, Sue Phillips, Joe Remenyi, Marguerite Robinson, Rich Rosenberg, Jim Roth, Orlanda Ruthven, Hans Seibel, Mike Slingsby, William Smith, William Steel, Astrid Ursem, J. D. Von Pischke, and David Wright. I have benefited from all of them, but while I am willing to share with them the credit for any virtues the book may have, I jealously guard my sole ownership of its faults.

Thousands of users and would-be users of financial services for the poor around the world have given their time to teach me how and why the existence and quality of financial services is important to them. Since it is hard to list or to thank them, I acknowledge my debt by dedicating this book to them.

Stuart Rutherford

CHAPTER 1
The need to save

Poor people get by on incomes that are small and irregular. But they often need sums of money larger than they have immediately to hand, to pay for life-cycle events such as birth, education, marriage, and death, for emergencies, and to seize opportunities to invest in assets or businesses. The only reliable and sustainable way to obtain these sums is to build them, somehow or other, from savings. Poor people have to save: and financial services for the poor are there to help them find ways to do so.

The poor as savers

A popular and useful definition of a poor person is some-one who does not have much money. Among academics, and in the aid industry, this definition has gone out of fashion.[1] But it suits my present purposes well, so I shall stick to it. In this book, when I talk about 'the poor', I mean people who, compared to their fellow citizens, don't have much money.

If you don't have much money it is especially important that you look after what money you have. But poor people are at a disadvantage in money management because the banks and insurance companies that serve the better-off rarely cater to the poor. Nevertheless, poor people do seek and find a wide variety of ways to better manage their money, as examples in this book will show. The book argues that we can learn a lot from the more successful money-managing efforts of the poor and use that learning to design new and better ways of bringing banking services to the slums and villages of the developing world.

Choosing to save...

Managing money well begins with hanging on to what you have. That means avoiding unnecessary expenditure and then finding a safe place to store whatever money is left over. Making that choice – the choice to save rather than to consume – is the foundation of money management.

Poor people run into problems with money management at this very first hurdle. If you live in an urban slum or in a straw hut in a village, finding a safe place to store savings is not easy. Coins buried in the earth or thrust into clay piggy banks, or paper money tucked into rafters or rolled inside hollowed-out bamboo, can be lost or stolen, blown away or may just rot. Certainly their value will decline, because of inflation. But the physical risks may be the least of the problem. Much tougher is keeping the cash safe from the many claims on it – claims by relatives or neighbours who have fallen on hard times, by hungry or sick children or alcoholic husbands, by your mother-in-law (who knows you have that secret hoard somewhere[2]) and by landlords, creditors and beggars. Finally, even when you do have a little cash left over at the day's end you'll most probably spend it in some trivial way unless you have somewhere safe to put it. I have lost count of the number of women who have told me how hard it is to save at home, and how much they would value a safe, simple way to save.

Nevertheless, the poor can save, do save, and want to save money. Only those so poor that they have left the cash economy altogether – elderly disabled people, for example, who live by begging food and firewood from neighbours – cannot save money. This book is not about them.

Can the poor really save?

The fact that the poor want to save and have some capacity to save is not self-evident. If you do not know much about how the poor organize their lives you may assume that the poor 'are too poor' to save. The poor spend all their income and still do not get enough to eat, so how can they save? The poor may need loans, but the last thing they need, you may think, is a savings service.[3]

By the time you have finished this book you should see that that is a misconception. But for the time being, notice that people (and not just the poor) may save money as it goes out (by, for example, keeping a few coins back from housekeeping money) as well as when it comes in (by deducting savings at source from wages or other income. Even the poorest, whether in the villages or in urban slums,[4] have to spend money frequently to buy basic items like food and fuel, and each time they do so brings an opportunity to save something, however tiny. Many poor housewives try to save in this way, even if their working husbands fail to save anything from their income.

That the poor do succeed in saving something is shown by their habit of lending each other small amounts of money (as well as small amounts of grain or kerosene or salt). In this 'reciprocal lending' I lend you a little money today – money that I have to spare and could have saved – on the understanding that you'll do the same for me at some other time. Among the poor in countries where studies have been done, this practice is more common than any other kind of financial transaction, and can account for an important fraction of the total value of all their transactions. In Bangladesh, for example, we found that they account for a quarter of the cash flow through financial transactions carried out by the poor.[5] The practice depends entirely on the poor's capacity and willingness to save.

Of course, poor people save in non-money ways too, and their 'in-kind' savings may be very important to them. This book is about managing *money*, and for that reason touches on non-cash savings only in this paragraph and the next. Poor people sometimes store their savings in livestock or other non-money ways simply because they haven't got access to a safe, rewarding, inflation-proof place to save money. Once they are given the opportunity, they may choose to convert some of their non-money savings into cash savings.[6] This is because cash savings can be less risky, and more useful, than non-money savings. Livestock, for example, a popular destination for non-money saving, may sicken and die or be stolen. Livestock is an inconveniently 'lumpy' way to save: if all you need is two dollars to buy medicine for a sick child, it is rather troublesome to have to sell a piglet worth thirty dollars.

Non-money savings are themselves easier to manage if you have access to a cash-savings service. After all, when you've sold the thirty-dollar piglet you need somewhere to put the twenty-eight dollars left over after buying the medicine. And if you save in the form of gold ornaments, as many poor people try to do, you will need a place to save up the cash you need to buy the ornament in the first place. Microfinance bank customers often use the services to save up or to borrow to buy, say, a gold earring. So a cash-savings service is useful even to people who prefer to store most of their savings in non-cash forms. As the world becomes ever more monetized many poor people are coming to see that, and the demand for financial services grows.

The poor, we have claimed, can and do save.[7] But why do they do so?

The poor as big spenders

You may not yet be fully convinced that the poor can and do (and want to) save. So we shall move on to the spending needs of the poor, which are less controversial.

Just because you're poor doesn't mean that all your expenditure will be in small sums. Much of it may be – you may buy only a little food or clothing at a time. But from time to time you need to spend large sums. How we classify those needs is a matter of choice. I like to list them in three main categories, 'life-cycle' events, emergency needs, and investment opportunities.

Life-cycle events

In Bangladesh and India, the dowry system makes marrying daughters an expensive matter. In parts of Africa, funerals can be very costly.[8] These are just two examples of 'life-cycle' events for which the poor need to amass large lump sums. Other such events include childbirth, education, home-building, widowhood and old-age generally, and the desire to bequeath money to heirs. Then there are the recurrent festivals like Eid, Christmas, or Diwali. In each case the poor need to be able to get their hands on sums of money which are much bigger than the amounts of cash which are normally found in the household. Many of these needs can be anticipated, even if their exact date is unknown. The awareness that such outlays are looming on the horizon is a source of great anxiety for many poor people.

Emergencies

Emergencies that create a sudden and unanticipated need for a large sum of money come in two forms – personal and impersonal. Personal emergencies include sickness or injury, the death of a bread-winner or the loss of employment, and theft or harassment. Impersonal ones include events such as war, floods, fires and cyclones, and – for slum dwellers – the bulldozing of their homes by the authorities. Again, you will be able to think of other examples. Each creates a sudden need for more cash than can normally be found at home. Finding a way to ensure access to cash when it is needed for these emergencies would help millions of poor people.

Opportunities

Besides innumerable *needs* for spending large sums of cash, there are also *opportunities* to spend. It may be possible to invest in an existing or new business, or to buy land or other productive assets. The lives of some poor people can be transformed if they can afford to pay a bribe to get a permanent job (perhaps in government service), or to pay for someone in the family to migrate to the city or overseas for well-paid work. The poor, like all of us, also like to invest in costly items that make life more comfortable – better roofing, better furniture, a water-pump, a fan, or a television. Stocking up on consumable items like rice is another investment that can save households a lot of money if they buy in bulk at cheaper prices.[9] One particular investment opportunity – setting up a new business or expanding an existing one – has attracted a lot of attention from the aid industry and from the new generation of banks that work with the poor.[10] But business investment is in fact just one of many needs and opportunities that require the poor to become occasional 'big spenders': we will return to it in Chapter Five.

Financial services for poor people

In this book we shall be concentrating on how the poor obtain the larger sums they need from time to time. We shall be reviewing the financial services – informal and formal – that have evolved to serve those needs. Of course, there are other services that poor people use that are 'financial' in the wider sense, such as those that ease the transmission or conversion of currency. Examples are sending money home from town or abroad. These services (important though they are for many poor people) are not dealt with in detail in this book.

So, to return to our main question: how are the poor to get hold of the usefully large lump sums they so often need? They might be lucky and have cash gifted to them, or be in some other way the beneficiary of charity – but this can hardly be relied on. It is not a sustainable way of getting access to large sums, at least for the great majority of the poor.

There are three common ways used by the poor to raise large sums. Where none of them are available the poor simply have to go without, an all-too-common outcome that can turn a temporary lack of liquidity into a household tragedy. The three common ways are:

- selling assets they already hold (or expect to hold)
- mortgaging (or 'pawning') those assets
- finding a way to turn savings into large lump sums

Let us review them.

Selling assets is a straightforward way of raising cash, though it isn't always easy to do it, especially if you're poor. It can be hard to find a buyer, and even if you find one, the price he or she offers you may not be attractive. Those, however, are not the main disadvantage of selling assets as a way of creating a lump sum: more serious is its unsustainability. Once the asset has been sold it's gone for good, and you need a savings service to help you build another lump sum in order to replace it. It is, therefore, normally a 'last resort' way of getting hold of money even though, for many poor people who lack financial services, it is regrettably common.

Note that poor people sometimes sell, in advance, assets that they don't hold now but expect to hold in the future. The most common rural example is the advance sale of crops. These 'advances' are, in effect, loans secured against yet-to-be harvested crops. The advance may be spent on financing the farming costs required to provide that crop.

But it may just as likely be used on any of the other needs and opportunities we reviewed in the previous section, or simply on surviving until harvest time.[11] This 'fungibility' of money, its ability to be turned into anything else, is one of its most useful features. Indeed, it is why we invented it.

The second method – mortgage and pawn – enables poor people to convert assets into cash and back again. It is the chance (not always realized) to regain the asset that distinguishes this second method from the first. Mortgaging (or pawning) allows the user to exploit their ownership of a stock of wealth by transforming it temporarily into cash. The most common examples are pawning gold at the pawn shop in town and mortgaging land in the countryside.[12]

These first two methods require that the users have assets, and poor people, almost by definition, have very few assets. This fact severely limits the effectiveness of these two methods, making them neither reliable nor sustainable. Only the third method is free of this limitation.

The third method enables poor people to convert their small savings into lump sums. This requires the users to have a flow of savings, however small or irregular. It allows them to exploit their capacity to make savings by offering a variety of mechanisms by which these savings can be transformed into lump sums.

Diagrams will make this clearer, I hope, so now is the time to introduce the first of the diagrams that are used in this book. In all the diagrams, time is represented by the horizontal axis, and value (of money) by the vertical axis.

Saving up

'Saving up' is the most obvious way to convert savings into lump sums. It allows a lump sum to be enjoyed in the future in exchange for a series of savings made now. Many poor people prefer this mechanism because it produces an 'unencumbered' lump sum – the lump sum is theirs to do what they like with once they have built it up. Its disadvantage is, as we have seen, that the poor find it hard to find a safe place to build their savings.

In Figure 1.1, savings made by the user are shown as negative values (below the horizontal line) since they are saved (deducted) from the saver's cash flow. The saved-up sum is shown as a positive value when it is 'withdrawn' and becomes available to be spent. Note that as soon as the sum is withdrawn, many savers like to start saving all over again: the diagram shows this possibility as two further saved sums on the right-hand side of the withdrawal.

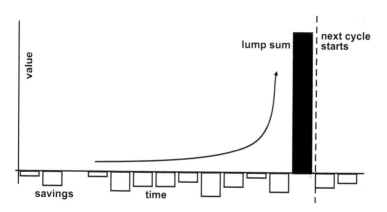

Figure 1.1 Saving up

Saving down

Another way to turn exactly the same series of savings into a lump sum, is to get someone to give you the lump sum first, as a loan, and then use the savings to repay the loan over time. Such loans can be thought of as 'advances against future savings'. This is what I call 'saving down' (Figure 1.2) – since it is the exact opposite of saving up. But just as the poor find it hard to find a safe place to save up, many of

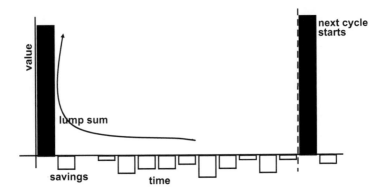

Figure 1.2 Saving down

them also find it very hard to find someone to help them 'save down'. Indeed, the most common complaint about moneylenders in developing countries is not that they charge extortionate rates of interest (though some do, of course) but that they are simply not available. As an Indian proverb has it, 'a good village is one with a good well and a good moneylender'.

Saving through

Finally we come to 'saving through', as shown in Figure 1.3, in which the saver goes on making a more or less continuous stream of savings that get converted to a lump sum at some intermediate point in time. Insurance policies do this: when you insure your car you make a series of savings (annual premiums or whatever) and take a lump sum back each time you crash into the gatepost and need to repair the bodywork. Not many poor people are insured – though many would dearly like to be – but other 'saving through' mechanisms are popular among them. They take the form of savings clubs of one sort or another and we shall look at them in detail in Chapter Three.

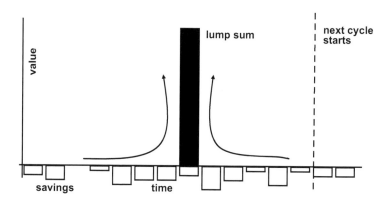

Figure 1.3 Saving through

No choice but to save... in whatever available way

Whichever way the poor find to turn their savings into lump sums – saving up, down or through – they *have* to save. The great irony of being poor is that you are 'too poor to save, but too poor not to save'. You may not be able to save much, but if you do not save at all you will have no way of getting hold of those 'usefully large lump sums' that you so often need. When the poor are not saving, it is rarely the case that they do not want or need to. More often it is due to the lack of a safe opportunity to save: no reliable place to save up, no friendly moneylender to help you save down, or no savings club or insurance plan to help you save through.

Which of these three methods you most often use may depend to a large extent on where you happen to live. For example, if you live in South Asia you are much more likely to use a moneylender than if you live in Africa, where there are not many moneylenders serving the poor. In West Africa there are many 'deposit collectors' – people who help you save up by collecting frequent small savings from you and then returning them to you when a lump sum has been formed, and many savings clubs which help you save through. East Africa also has many savings clubs but very few deposit collectors. So to create their lump sums, South Asians are more likely to save down, West Africans to save up and East Africans to save through. This oddity strengthens my belief that money lending, deposit collecting, and savings clubs are devices that may look very different but are in fact all essentially doing the same job – the job of helping poor people turn their savings into usefully large lump sums.

Basic personal financial intermediation[13]

The set of mechanisms I call saving up, down and through needs a name that is less clumsy than 'services which enable poor people to convert their small savings into usefully large lump sums'. I suggest the term 'basic personal financial intermediation'. I admit this is still a mouthful, but it does describe the process at work.

The process is one of 'financial intermediation' in the sense that a regular banker would recognize,[14] because many small savings are 'intermediated' ('carried across') into lump sums. But the process is 'personal' because we are talking about how one poor person can turn her savings into a lump sum for her own use (whereas bankers normally talk about intermediating the savings of many into loans for a few – who may be entirely different people). Finally I call the process 'basic' because it is a basic requirement of everyday life for most poor people. Some poor people enjoy access to more complex financial services, but virtually everybody needs the 'basic' services that we focus on in this book.

Organization of the book

This introductory chapter has laid out the basic argument of the book.

The second chapter illustrates 'saving up, saving down and saving through' by means of real examples from the slums and villages of the developing world.

Chapters Three and Four are devoted to detailed descriptions of the various kinds of informal financial services for the poor, while Chapter Five takes a summary look at microfinance institutions – the new banks that are getting steadily better at providing banking services for poor customers.

The last chapter, Chapter Six, offers an understanding of how poor people manage their money from a different view, based on research in which the financial lives of selected poor people are studied in detail over a period of a full year. The chapter ends with some principles that we should keep in mind when planning better financial services for the poor.

Conclusion

We end the chapter with a summary of the book's basic argument.

Financial Services for Poor People[15]

- Financial services for poor people are there mainly to help them get hold of usefully large sums of cash for spending or investing.
- Assets (stocks) can be sold to raise cash, but this method is limited by the fact that the poor hold few assets.
- Mortgaging or pawning assets (exchanging them temporarily for cash) is an important financial service for the poor, but once again it is limited by their lack of assets.
- The only reliable and sustainable way of raising lump sums of cash is to find a way of building them from your capacity to save small amounts from time to time. I have called this method 'basic personal financial intermediation'. It may take the form of:

- o *Saving up*: where you accumulate savings first and take the resulting lump sum later;
- o *Saving down*: where you take the lump sum first as an advance (or loan) against future savings; or
- o *Saving through*: where you to take a lump sum at the time it is needed in exchange for a continuous stream of savings or some combination of any two or all three of these.
- In each case, saving is the essential ingredient, and the devices and services are the ways of converting savings into usefully large lump sums.

That is why the poor need to save.

In the next chapter we provide practical examples of how poor people build lump sums from savings.

CHAPTER 2
Three ways to save

There are many devices and services that allow the poor to save up, save down, or save through. But they are unevenly distributed across and within nations and populations, and many poor people have limited access to them. As a result, where they can be found they are in high demand, and the poor are prepared to pay high prices or to accept high levels of risk to get them, or to put a lot of effort into organizing them for themselves.

Of the propositions that I put forward in the first chapter, the ones that people usually find most strange are the ideas that:

- most poor people want to save, can save, and do save; and
- loans are often nothing more than one way of turning savings into lump sums.

This chapter is devoted to a small number of examples of 'basic personal financial intermediation' that will, I hope, make these ideas feel less odd. Each example is a real one that I have investigated for myself by observing and talking to the people involved.[1] All except the last example are of 'informal' services and devices, and are typical of phenomena that are widespread among the poor all over the developing world, and have been for many decades, even though details vary from place to place and time to time. The growth over the last three decades of 'microfinance', or organized financial services for poor people, is changing things for many people, though they are still a minority of the world's poor. We will look at microfinance in Chapter Five.

Saving up: Deposit collectors

The need to find a safe place to keep savings is so strong that some poor people willingly pay others to take their savings out of their hands and store them.

We begin with 'saving up' and we start our journey in India, in the slums of the south-eastern city of Vijayawada. There Sukhwinder Arora and I found Jyothi doing her rounds. Jyothi is a middle-aged, part-educated woman who makes her living as a peripatetic (mobile) deposit collector. Her clients are slum dwellers, mostly women. Jyothi has, over the years, built a good reputation as a safe pair of hands that can be trusted to take care of the savings of her clients.

This is how she works. She gives each of her clients a simple card, divided into 220 cells (eleven rows and twenty columns), as shown in Figure 2.1. Her clients commit themselves to saving a certain amount of money, regularly, over

5	5	5	5	5	5	5	5	5	5	5	5	5	5	5	5	5	5	5	5
5	5	5	5	5	5	5	5	5	5	5	5	5	5	5	5	5	5	5	5
5	5	5	5	5	5	5													

Figure 2.1 Jyothi's savings card

time. For example, a client may agree to save five rupees (Rs5) a day for 220 days, completing one cell each day. At the end of the period she will have deposited 220 times Rs5, or Rs1,100 (that was about US$25 at the time I met Jyothi). Having made this agreement, it is Jyothi's duty to visit her client each day to collect the five rupees. In the card reproduced here the client has got as far as saving forty-seven times, for a total of Rs235 to date.

When the contract is fulfilled – that is when the client has handed Rs5 to Jyothi 220 times (which may actually take more or less than 220 days, because slum dwelling women are human beings and not slot machines) – the client takes her savings back. However, she does not get back the full amount, since Jyothi needs to be paid for the service she provides. These fees vary from one deposit collector to another, but in Jyothi's case it is 20 out of the 220 cells, or Rs100 out of the Rs1,100 saved up by the client in our example.

We can calculate Jyothi's fee as a percentage of the cash she handles, in which case her fee, at Rs100 in Rs1,100, is 9 per cent. For a relatively short-term contract like Jyothi's that is probably the best way of thinking about the cost of the service.[2] Alternatively, if we want to compare what she gets with what a formal bank might offer its clients, we can work out the annualized interest rate[3] that her savers are earning on their savings. Obviously, since they get back *less* than they put in, they are earning a *negative* interest rate, but what is that rate?

In our example, Jyothi's client saved Rs1,100 over 220 days. That means that *on average* over the 220 day period she had half that amount, or Rs550, deposited with Jyothi. On those Rs550 she has 'earned' minus Rs100, or minus18 per cent. Minus 18 per cent over a 220-day period is roughly equal to minus 30 per cent over 365 days. So the annualized rate is about *minus* 30 per cent.[4]

Why should savers be prepared to accept a negative interest rate on savings? We can give two sorts of answers,

which complement each other. One comes from economists. They would say 'these rates are so abnormal that
there is obviously an imperfect market here'. They mean
that the *demand* for savings services is not being freely
matched by the *supply* of savings services. That applies to
Vijayawada's slums. Even though some slum dwellers live
within a stone's throw of a formal bank, banks are cultural-
ly too remote to attract them, and don't like to accept tiny
deposits like five rupees a day. Apart from people like Jyothi, slum dwellers have very few other places to put their
savings. It is extremely hard to save at home, as we noted
in the first chapter. Competitors for Jyothi are few, perhaps
because it takes a long time and a special sort of person to
build up the reputation for safety that Jyothi has done.

The second answer comes from the users of this system,
and sheds light on the nature of their demand for savings
services. The first client I talked to was doing it to save up
for school fees and clothing for her two school-aged children. She knew she had to have about Rs800 in early July,
or she would miss out on getting her children into school.
Her husband, a day labourer, could not be relied on to come
up with so much money at one time, and in any case he
felt that looking after the children's education was *her* duty,
not his. She knew she would not be able to save so large
an amount at home – with so many other more immediate demands on the scarce cash she wouldn't be able to
maintain the discipline. I asked her if she understood that
she was paying 30 per cent a year for the privilege of saving
with Jyothi. She said she knew she was paying a lot, but
still thought it a bargain. Without Jyothi, she wouldn't be
able to send the children to school. Other users told similar
stories, and dwellers in a neighbouring slum, where there is
no Jyothi at work, envied Jyothi's clients.

These ideas also help us understand why poor people
tolerate the *risk* of handing their savings to an unlicensed
collector. In the absence of safe ways to save, a risky way is
better than no way at all. A paper prepared for *MicroSave*,

an initiative that promotes good financial services for poor people, found from surveys in East Africa that almost all poor people they interviewed had lost savings and that, as you would expect, losses were greater in the 'informal sector' (which includes deposit takers like Jyothi) than in formal banks – though one in seven of their interviewees reported they had lost savings in formal banks (Wright and Mutesasira 2002). Poor people are aware of risk, but have to accept it. The paper argues that any attempt by authorities to ban informal sector savings would be a serious mistake. The authors write that 'poor people cannot wait for the perfect system to protect their deposits'. In this and the next two chapters we will see some of the ways that informal systems help to lessen risk.

In terms of the concept of 'basic personal financial intermediation', we can say that Jyothi's clients commit themselves to a series of equal and (more or less) regular but tiny *savings* which Jyothi holds for them until they are transformed (intermediated) into a usefully large lump sum (large enough to pay the school costs, for example). We can represent Jyothi's service by using a diagram of the type described in the first chapter. Obviously, Jyothi offers a saving up service, but we need to modify the 'saving up' diagram to take account of two things: the fee (or interest) that Jyothi charges, and the fact that she accepts equal (not unequal) deposit values.

Jyothi's savings service is shown in Figure 2.2. We can show the savings and the fees below the horizontal axis, as negative values, since the client pays these *in* to Jyothi, and the lump sum above the axis, as a positive value, since the client gets this *out* of the system.

Note one more thing about services like Jyothi's: clients often start a second cycle as soon as the first cycle is finished. That is why there is a broken vertical line after the pay-out, to indicate the end of one cycle and the beginning of the next.

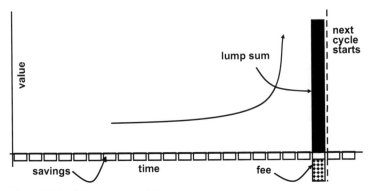

Figure 2.2 Jyothi's savings model

We can sum up Jyothi's service as follows:

- The market for savings deposit in slums is 'imperfect' (demand is not matched by supply).
- Slum dwellers want to turn their savings into lump sums for many different needs and opportunities.
- Unable to save at home, and unable to use remote unfriendly banks, they accept the risk of entrusting their savings to unlicensed, informal, peripatetic collectors.
- When they find one that they can trust, time and time again, they are willing to pay a high price (as much as 30 per cent a year) to have that collector take away their savings and store them safely until needed.
- The service that these deposit collectors render represents the simplest version of 'basic personal financial intermediation' for poor people.

We look next at one of Jyothi's competitors, the urban moneylender.

Saving Down: The Urban Moneylender

In an environment where the demand for savings services far outstrips supply, it is not surprising that many loans to poor people turn out to be just another way of turning savings into lump sums, through the mechanism I call 'saving down'.

There are many kinds of moneylender.[5] There is one kind that is common in many urban slums of the sort where deposit collectors like Jyothi work. Indeed, I have taken my example from Vijayawada again because I want to draw a comparison with Jyothi. I got to know this moneylender's clients in a slum just over the railway tracks from the one where Jyothi works.

His working method is simple. He gives loans to poor people without any security (or 'collateral'), and then takes back his money in regular instalments over the next few weeks or months. He charges for this service by deducting a percentage (in his case 15 per cent) of the value of the loan at the time of disbursal. One of his clients reported the deal to me as follows.

'I run a very small shop' (it's a small timber box on stilts on the sidewalk inside which he squats and sells a few basic household goods) 'and I need his service to help me maintain my stock of goods. I take Rs1,000 from him, but he immediately deducts Rs150, so I get Rs850 in my hand. He then visits me weekly and I pay him Rs100 a week for ten weeks. As soon as I have finished he normally lets me repeat'.

This client, Ramalu, showed me the scruffy bit of card that the moneylender had given him and on which his weekly repayments are recorded. It was quite like the cards Jyothi hands out. There are many other similarities between Jyothi and the moneylender. We can see that if we redraw our diagram to show this moneylender's system (see Figure 2.3).

The main difference, the fact that the pay-out comes first, as a loan, is immediately apparent. But let us look at the similarities. In each case the client is using the service to swap a series of small regular pay-ins (or savings) for a usefully big pay-out. In other words, these are both forms

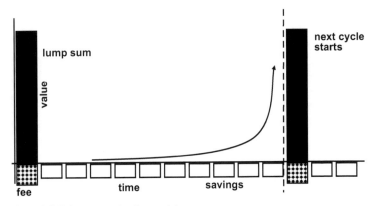

Figure 2.3 Urban moneylender model

of 'basic personal financial intermediation'. With the urban moneylender, the pay-out comes first, and can be understood as an advance against future savings, as is true of many loans to poor people.

Another similarity is that clients often continue to a second cycle, and then a third and so on. When you have completed several cycles it doesn't make much difference whether in the *first* cycle the loan or the savings came first – one may not even be able to remember. Indeed, when we first met Ramalu it took us a few minutes to work out whether he was using a deposit collector or a moneylender: Ramalu himself wasn't clear. Every day (or week or month) a small *pay-in* is made and every now and then (every 220 days or every ten weeks) a usefully big *pay-out* arrives. This is just what the poor need, as we saw earlier in the chapter. This is the essence of 'basic personal financial intermediation'.

As in all cases of 'basic personal financial intermediation', the value of the pay-out is directly linked to the value of the pay-ins. In the case of Jyothi, the client decides these values, by choosing how much to pay-in per cell. In the case of the moneylender, the moneylender makes the decision, by determining the value of the loan (or at least its *maximum* value), and the schedule by which it is to be repaid. To do this, he has to judge the client's capacity to save, and in this he is often helped by a history of previous similar deals with the same client or with people in similar situations.

This brings us to another important difference between the two services: their price. Ramalu's moneylender's service is considerably more expensive than Jyothi's saving up service. Calculating his rates as a simple 'fee for the amount transacted' in the way we did for Jyothi, we can see that the moneylender charges 15 per cent of the cash he handles (as opposed to Jyothi's 9 per cent). We can estimate the *annualized* interest rate using a rule-of-thumb similar to the one we used for Jyothi. Ramalu had an average loan in his pocket of Rs425 for the ten week period, on which he paid Rs150 interest. Rs150 is 35 per cent of Rs425, so dividing 35 by 10 weeks and multiplying by 52 weeks brings us to an annual rate of 180 per cent, again much higher than Jyothi's rate. More formal conventions for calculating annual interest rates would arrive at an even higher figure, but given the relatively short term of Ramalu's loan contract our rule-of-thumb is not unsuitable.[6]

The client pays the moneylender more but of course gets more for his (or her) money. For one thing, the moneylender accepts the risk that the client may be unable or unwilling to make the pay-ins, a risk which Jyothi doesn't face (her clients have to accept the risk that *she'll* run off with *their* money). Secondly, the moneylender puts up the initial finance for the first cycle, whereas Jyothi needs no capital to run her business. Thirdly, the moneylender has to use his judgement about the maximum value of each contract, while Jyothi can happily leave that to her clients. For all these reasons clients pay the moneylender more than Jyothi for an essentially similar 'basic personal financial intermediation' service. We can now see why women in nearby slums envied Jyothi's clients their access to a safe and relatively cheap way of building a lump sum from their savings.

Summing up the Urban Moneylender's service:

- An alternative to Jyothi's saving up services, as a way to turn savings into lump sums, is to promise someone to use those same savings to repay an advance.

- This is likely to be more expensive, since the moneylender has more decisions to make than Jyothi does, has to take a greater initial risk, and has to supply initial capital.

- When clients use either Jyothi's or the moneylender's service cycle after cycle, the distinction between 'saving' and 'borrowing' disappears: in both cases a pattern is created of swapping small pay-ins for occasional pay-outs.

Saving Through: The Merry-go-round

But both sets of clients, Jyothi's and the moneylender's, could run the same sort of service for themselves, for free. To see how, we need to look at Rotating Savings and Credit Associations, or ROSCAs, which are saving-through devices. Since there are many kinds of ROSCA we'll look at a very simple one in this chapter; the 'merry-go-round' as it is practised in the slums of Nairobi, Kenya.[7]

Mary, a woman who's ROSCA I studied there, is, like Ramalu, a very small vendor. She sells vegetables from a shelf set in the window of her hut. She is one of 15 members of her merry-go-round. This is what they do.

Every day, day-in day-out, each of them saves 100 shillings. So each day a total of 1,500 shillings is saved (about $40 when I met Mary). Each day one of the fifteen women takes the full 1,500 shillings. After each of the fifteen women has taken the 'prize' in turn, which takes fifteen days of course, the cycle starts again. Mary was 'serial number 7' in the cycle. So seven days after the start of the first cycle, and then once every fifteen days, she gets 1,500 shillings in return for 100 shillings put in each and every day. Mary told me she had been in this merry-go-round with the same fellow-members for two and half years.

Figure 2.4 shows Mary's merry-go-round where the 'basic personal financial intermediation' function and its relationship to Jyothi and the moneylender is clear.

The 'do-it-yourself' nature of this device gives it its particular advantage over the other examples. There are no fees or interest payments. You get back exactly what you put in. Of course, there are other, non-monetary costs. Mary and her friends have to organize their merry-go-round, maintain trust and agree among themselves the number of members and the size and frequency of the pay-ins. None of these tasks need to be done if you use a commercial provider like Jyothi or the moneylender.

But if you 'get back exactly what you put in' then what is the point? The point is to transform many small savings into a single usefully large sum. That so many poor people round the world, like Mary, do this every day is strong evidence of the importance of that basic task.

Mary takes her merry-go-round very seriously. The total value of the stock of her 'shop' is only a little over 1,500

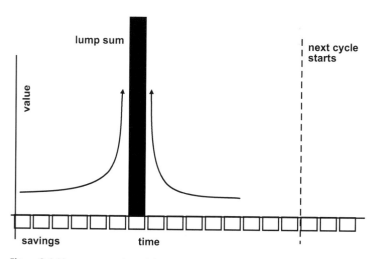

Figure 2.4 Merry-go-round model

shillings. Often, Mary has to dig into her working capital to pay for extra costs for her two children (Mary has no husband). But she can do so safe in the knowledge that, provided she is faithful to her merry-go-round, she'll get a 1,500 shilling lump sum within the next fortnight, and can then re-capitalize her shop. She once joined an 'NGO' that offered a bigger loan, but she found that its repayment schedule was too long to suit her needs, so she left. Instead, she joined another, longer-period ROSCA which she uses to build up her savings over a longer term, for use in schooling her boys.

Many ROSCA members in Nairobi join more than one ROSCA. This helps them get around a disadvantage of ROSCAs, an inflexibility in which everyone has to save the same amount in the same period, whereas individual households will have actual needs that vary in quantity and timing. There are ways of adapting ROSCAs to avoiding this disadvantage, as we shall see in Chapter Three where we take a closer look at them.

Summing up Mary's ROSCA:

- ROSCAs perform the same job as Jyothi's saving up service and the moneylender's saving down service: they turn savings into lump sums.
- But they do it as a club of equals rather than as service provider and client.
- The advantage is that that the service has no monetary cost, though it does place a management burden on the members.
- The very fact that 'you get back exactly what you put in' proves how important the basic intermediation of savings into a lump sum is for poor people.
- Mary's type of ROSCA, the merry-go-round, treats everyone the same, so it isn't good at satisfying individual needs. Members get round that by joining several merry-go-rounds at once. The critical variables are the

number of members, the frequency and the value of the pay-ins.

Another way of getting round the difficulty of meeting individual needs in a club of equals is to run a 'fund', which is what we look at next.

Saving Up and Down: Rabeya's 'fund'

Is it possible to devise a type of 'basic personal financial intermediation' device that includes most of the advantages and eliminates most of the disadvantages of deposit collectors, moneylenders and ROSCAs? The last two examples in this chapter show two attempts to do so.

We start with what the slum-dwellers of Dhaka, in Bangladesh, call a 'fund' (Rutherford 1997). This is a type of savings club that can be found all over the world. In many places, including Dhaka, it is the main alternative to the ROSCA among user-owned devices for 'basic personal financial intermediation'. It differs from a ROSCA in that the savings deposited by its members accumulate in a 'fund' from which members may borrow, though only if they wish to. Figure 2.5 illustrates such a fund.

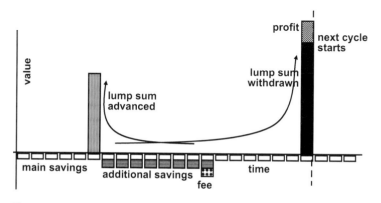

Figure 2.5 Rabeya's fund

In the figure for the 'fund' both a 'saving-up' and a 'saving-down' element are visible. The series of regular pay-ins below the line provides the big payout at the end – a classic saving up pattern. But you can also see an advance (above the line) against a series of additional pay-ins below the line, representing the saving down device. Figure 2.5 is more complicated than earlier figures, and this reflects one of the disadvantages of funds: they require more deliberate and careful management to make them work well. What follows is a brief description of how they work, based on what happened to a fund that I tracked for some months in Dhaka.

There were 23 members in the fund, and all of them had committed themselves to save on a weekly basis for one year, after which the fund was to close. Each member chose how much to save, but it was always some multiple of 10 taka (at that time worth about 20 cents US). In practice, some saved 10, some 20 and a few were saving 50 taka a week (shown below the line in the diagram as 'main savings'). As they came in, these savings were stored with Rabeya, the fund's chairperson, who locked them in a steel cupboard in her living room. Although a housewife, she had run many funds in her neighbourhood, where she was well known. She kept a simple set of accounts in a school exercise book.

As soon as this cash-in-hand became big enough, members with a need or an opportunity for a lump sum were allowed to borrow from it (shown above the line in the diagram as 'lump sum advanced'). The terms of these loans were straightforward: the borrower had to pay interest of 5 per cent a month, and had to repay the loan before the end of the year (repayments and interest on loans are shown below the line in the diagram). According to the fund's rules, decisions about who took this chance to 'save down' and how much they took were made by the members collectively. In practice the Chairperson had by far the biggest say. She strove to make sure that everyone who wanted a loan could get one, and that no member borrowed an amount that was beyond what Rabeya estimated they could repay (or 'save down') in the time allowed.

At the end of the year, the total amount in the fund, including the interest earned on the loans made from it, was put on the table and shared by the members in proportion to the savings they had made. It worked out that for each 10 taka saved per week, members got back 580 taka (shown as 'lump sum withdrawn and profit' in the diagram). Thus a member saving at the rate of 10 taka a week saved 520 in the year (52 weeks) and got a 'profit'[8] of 60 taka. Members got this profit on their savings irrespective of whether they took a loan.

How did this fund perform in comparison with other devices, in its costs and rewards? Compared to the moneylender, the fund's advances are, at 5 per cent a month (about 60 per cent a year[9] instead of 180 per cent), a much cheaper way of borrowing lump sums. As a way of saving up, the fund is not only cheaper than saving with Jyothi, it returns a good profit. If you save 10 taka a week, or 520 a year, you get back 580 taka, or 11.5 per cent more than you put in, instead of losing 9 per cent as with Jyothi. This is an annual rate of plus 23 per cent (instead of minus 30 per cent with Jyothi).[10] As with Jyothi you can choose how much to save each week but you do not get a daily visit, and you can't choose your own start date, since that is a decision that has to be made collectively. But best of all, the fund offers you *two* ways of swapping small pay-ins for lump sums, instead of one. You save up and withdraw, but if you wish you can save down by taking an advance as well. This double opportunity makes the fund more flexible than the ROSCA, at the cost of more paperwork and management.

The added management burden makes funds less transparent and more vulnerable to fraud than ROSCAs. Some conditions help to minimize this risk. For example, in places where funds are very common, the relationship between the amount users pay in and the amount they receive at the end tends to become fixed, so that almost every fund in the area charges the same rate for loans and guarantees the same minimum return on savings. This 'institutionalization' of funds makes it easier for illiterate (and literate) people to know exactly what they're getting themselves into.

Not all funds are time-bound in the way that Rabeya's was. Some go on for an indefinite period. But being time-bound is a very healthy feature that good funds share with ROSCAs, which are naturally time-bound. During a ROSCA, or at the end of a time-bound fund, either you get your money back or you don't. If their ROSCAs or funds don't work properly, the members walk away and the device dies. I call this an 'action audit' and it substitutes very well for the sort of formal but less easily understandable audit that professional savings banks get accountants to do. As a result of this 'action audit' function, poor club chairpersons are soon out of a job, and members flock to others with a sound record. This doesn't ensure that most savings clubs are well run, but it does ensure, at least, that badly run ones disappear quickly.

Funds can be wholly user-owned (run by the people that use them, as in Rabeya's case), or run by club officers on behalf of users, as when a church or social club runs them. They can also be run professionally, and some bigger church and trade-association funds are more or less 'commercial' in that they charge for the service and generate a surplus, ensuring their continuity. We shall look at some examples in the third chapter.

Summing up Rabeya's fund:

- 'Funds' combine saving up and saving down in one club.
- For this reason they are potentially more useful and more flexible than ROSCAs, since members can engage in both forms of personal intermediation at a

time, and can vary the amounts they save up or save
down.

- Because the fee charged on the 'saving down' pays for
  interest paid out on the 'saving up', funds offer a profitable way to save when compared to Jyothi.
- Because the fees (or interest) charged on saving down
  returns to the members in the form of profit on their
  saving up, funds are cheaper to use than an urban
  moneylender.
- But funds need more management, making them
  more prone to fraud and misunderstandings than
  simple ROSCAs.
- There are however several ways of reducing these risks:
  having a fixed and fairly short term, followed by the
  'action audit' is one of the most important.

Our last example in this chapter is commercially run,
and is a deliberate attempt to sum up many of the lessons
of 'basic personal financial intermediation'.

Saving Up and Down, Over Short and Long Terms, with Variable Payments: *Safe*Save

If we review the examples shown so far (Jyothi, the moneylender, the ROSCA and the fund) in the light of what
was said in the first chapter regarding the financial service
needs of the poor, we shall find two ways in which the circumstances and needs of the poor are still not being met.

Firstly, we noted that poor people need to store savings
for the long run, for widowhood or old age or for their
heirs.[11] None of the examples shown so far helps them to
do this (or at least not directly).

Secondly, we noted that poor people's ability to save fluc-
tuates with time, so that they may be able to save a lot in
one week and very little in another. But in all our examples
so far, there is the requirement for (more or less) *fixed* saving at a *fixed* interval (the same sum each day for each cell

on Jyothi's card or for Mary's ROSCA, or for each week for the moneylender or for Rabeya's fund).

Both of these shortcomings are difficult for the *very* poor (Rutherford 1998). It is the very poor who suffer most hardship in old age and most need financial protection for the end of their lives. Many poor people get excluded from these devices – and often indeed *exclude themselves* – out of anxiety that they won't be able to save the same amount *every* day (or week, or month) for a *whole* year (or other period).

*Safe*Save is an MFO (microfinance organization) that I founded in Dhaka, Bangladesh, in 1996 that is designed to overcome these two shortcomings. Figure 2.6 shows how.

*Safe*Save employs Collectors (field staff) who visit each client every day at their home or workplace. They provide the same *opportunity* to save (or repay) that Jyothi and daily ROSCAs do. On each occasion, clients may save, but in any amount they like, including zero. The 'main savings' in the diagram show this: they vary over time. From this accumulation of savings clients may *withdraw* a lump sum at any time they like, as shown by the 'short-term sum withdrawn'. Then, as in a fund, they can take optional advanc-

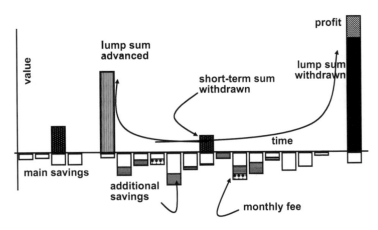

Figure 2.6 *Safe*Save, Bangladesh

es, but, better than a fund, clients repay when they like and can take as long as they like provided they pay the interest (shown as 'monthly fee') each month. Finally, as in a fund, they get a pay-out of their accumulated savings plus profits. But unlike time-bound funds, they can leave these savings on deposit for as long as they like and earn more profit the longer they leave them in. The only respect in which this flexibility is compromised is that if they are borrowing then their withdrawals from savings cannot cause their savings balance to fall below one-third of the outstanding value of their loan (in effect, *Safe*Save secures a third of the loan against savings).

The current version of *Safe*Save running in the slums of Dhaka, Bangladesh in 2009 pays clients about 6 per cent a year on savings (much less than Rabeya's fund and similar to what formal banks pay) and charges 3 per cent a month on advances (less than Rabeya's fund but more than formal banks).

*Safe*Save, now more than twelve years old, runs profitably, but has grown slowly, not because of lack of demand (its services are popular) but because Bangladesh offers no fully satisfactory legal identity for its operations, and growth must wait until new laws are in place. No more will be said on *Safe*Save here, since this chapter is concerned with 'basic personal financial intermediation' and focuses on the user's perspective.[12]

The main question raised by *Safe*Save in that context is *discipline*.

We have already seen that without discipline it is hard to save. This is true whether those savings are made 'down', following an advance against savings (as with moneylenders), or whether they precede a withdrawal or advance (as with a deposit collector like Jyothi) or are made both before and after a withdrawal/advance (as in a ROSCA). Moneylenders enforce discipline by their regular weekly visit, and Jyothi does it by daily appearances on the doorsteps of her clients. ROSCAs fail if their self-imposed discipline falters.

*Safe*Save is no different, except that it has given up two things that undeniably promote discipline very strongly – *uniformity* of deposit size, and *regularity* of deposit. In all the other examples shown, so far, the user pays a set amount at a set interval. In *Safe*Save the user may pay at any interval and in any amount, including zero.

The risk is, therefore, that without any compulsion to pay a set sum at a set interval, *Safe*Save's clients will simply fail to save. *Safe*Save's experimental aspect is precisely that it is testing the extent to which a *frequent and reliable opportunity* to save is a way of maintaining savings *discipline*. So far, the indications are good. It looks as if the frequent opportunity to save – having someone knock on your door each day – is as good, or even better, as a way of maximizing savings, as the obligation to pay a set sum at a set interval.

Summing up *Safe*Save:

- *Safe*Save is a deliberate attempt to set up a financial service scheme for the poor which meets their circumstances and needs as understood by this author over twenty-five years of research and practice.
- It allows for the fact that the poor can save and want to save, but can save only in small (but variable sized) amounts and cannot save each and *every* day.
- It allows for the fact that the poor need to turn those savings into usefully large lump sums at both short and long-term notice, and sometimes without notice. It recognizes that to help them do this it must provide them, on a daily basis:
  o The chance to save up (to save and withdraw)
  o The chance to save down (to take an advance against *future* savings)
  o The opportunity to store up savings for long-term needs
- *Safe*Save recognizes that no-one can save without discipline, and offers a *daily opportunity* to save to all its

clients as a way of developing and maintaining that discipline.

- *Safe*Save is thus the most *flexible* of all the examples dealt with in this chapter, and because of this it attracts the *very* poor who can be frightened off by the need to pay set sums at set intervals.

Conclusion

This chapter has used actual examples to illustrate 'basic personal financial intermediation', the process through which people turn their savings into usefully large lump sums of money. Poor people need this process as much as anyone else, because poor people *can* save and poor people have frequent need, throughout their lives, of 'usefully large lump sums of money'. Other ways of getting hold of large sums of cash, such as being the beneficiary of charity, or selling or pawning assets, are either unreliable or unsustainable. The task of financial services for the poor, therefore, is to provide mechanisms through which the swap from savings into lump sums can be made.

As an introduction to the wide variety of such mechanisms, the chapter has described three informal devices. Deposit collectors will accept people's savings and return a lump sum to them, moneylenders will provide the lump sum up front and then collect savings in repayment, and ROSCAs allow people to get together to make savings from which each in turn takes their lump sum. Elements from these three systems can be combined to provide a more flexible service, as we saw in the example of Rabeya's fund.

These devices are all time-bound, but poor people's needs for 'basic personal financial intermediation' are never-ending, so many poor people engage in cycle after cycle with their deposit collector, money lender, ROSCA, or fund. *Safe*Save, the last example in the chapter, illustrates one way of serving poor people's longer term needs for swaps, by allowing them to keep money on deposit for the long term. *Safe*Save, unlike the other devices discussed so far, allows savings deposits to be made as and when the saver has them to hand: the idea behind this flexibility is that the *very* poor, who may feel unable to save set sums at set intervals, can also avail of the service.

CHAPTER 3

Informal devices: ROSCAs and ASCAs

Savings clubs are groups of people who run their own basic financial services. In some of them, members come together just to support each other with their individual saving. But other clubs take advantage of the fact that, as the members' savings grow, some or all of them can take and use some of that money. There are two main kinds of these 'sharing'[1] clubs: the ROSCA (where everyone puts in and takes out the same amount, in rotation) and the ASCAs (where some may use the money during the life of the club, and others not).

The world of money management for the poor is diverse and complex. Devices and services have long histories, and there are countless variations. Regions have developed solutions tailored to their particular social and economic conditions. As a result, it is not easy to categorise financial services for the poor. Nevertheless, this chapter and the next divide informal services into two main groups – *savings clubs* in this chapter, and *managers and providers* in the next. The classification, which is based on who owns and manages the services, isn't water-tight, but is robust enough to be useful.

Savings clubs are owned and managed by their users, or members. In this chapter we will describe 'saving-up' clubs, where members save individually and come together just to give each other encouragement in the hard task of saving, and then, in greater detail, two kinds of club where members make use of their savings as they go along. One is the ROSCA type, where the cash rotates evenly between all the group members (as in Mary's merry-go-round). The other is the 'accumulating' type where some members may borrow while others don't (as in Rabeya's fund). For the accumulating (fund) type I am going to use the name that Fritz Bouman gave them: the ASCA, for Accumulating Saving and Credit Association.[2]

Managers run savings clubs for other people, either for profit or as a social service, and *providers* are actors such as Jyothi and the urban moneylender that we met in the previous chapter: people who provide services to others, usually for profit. We will look at them in the next chapter. Box 3.1 sets out this classification.

At the end of the chapter is a section on the ingenious *'ubbu-tungnguls'* of northern Philippines. It shows the inventiveness of poor people when it comes to managing money, and reminds us how hard it can be to categorize their inventions.

The saving-up club

The simplest savings clubs are those where members make their individual savings without ever sharing them. In theory they could do this on their own, without forming a club, but the fact that so many do form a club shows how

Box 3.1 Classes of basic personal financial intermediation services				
Savings Clubs (owner-managed) [this chapter]			Managers [chapter four]	Providers [chapter four]
Saving-up clubs (where members save individually)	ROSCAs (where the savings are shared and rotate evenly between members)	ASCAs (where the savings are shared and can be borrowed unevenly by the members)	Includes religious and welfare organizations, and 'chit' managers	Includes deposit collectors, moneylenders, and pawnbrokers

hard it is to save on your own. Clubs of this sort are often very informal indeed, without written rules or officers. The members may already know each other through some other activity – mothers of schoolchildren, perhaps, or friends that meet at the same tea-stall or workplace. The club helps them in their saving by reinforcing the discipline that we discussed at the close of the previous chapter. Members jog each other's memory and create some gentle 'peer pressure', to help ensure that the savings get made. Sometimes, everyone saves similar amounts, on the same day each week, and everyone takes their savings back on the same day: none of this is necessary to make the club function, but it all helps to strengthen the discipline. Often the club is aimed at a particular time of year when everyone needs a lump sum, like the Eid, Christmas or Diwali festivals we mentioned in Chapter One as 'life cycle events' that cause the need to save. These clubs seem to work best if the period over which members save is quite short, usually no more than a year, since the longer the money is held on account and the bigger it grows, the more risk there is of its being lost or stolen or embezzled. This is especially so where a club member, such as a treasurer, holds the money at home, and that is why members try to get their savings out of their own hands, often by opening a joint bank account.[3]

Fire insurance clubs

Sometimes, user-managed saving-up clubs are more structured and longer-term. An example is the 'fire insurance society' found in the slums of Dhaka, Bangladesh. Dhaka's slums are highly combustible. The houses and shops have woven bamboo walls, they sit cheek to jowl, and cooking is done inside, over open fires. It needs only a moment of inattention, or a naughty child, to set them ablaze. Once a fire has set in, it is likely to wipe out dozens of homes and shops at a time. Since there is no public compensation for residents and shopkeepers who lose out in such fires, some slums have devised a form of self-help insurance that is, in essence, a saving-up club.

In these clubs, residents (or sometimes just the shop-keepers in the bazaar-section of the slum) agree to save a set sum each week (or a multiple thereof) which is collected by a cashier and banked. In the event of a fire, the fund is withdrawn and distributed to members in proportion to their contribution. Figure 3.1 shows a fire insurance society from the point of view of an individual user.

Nothing could be simpler. The pay-out equals the total of the contributions paid in by the member at the time of the fire. Bank interest is used to cover the expenses of running the scheme, so the user earns no interest. Because it is important to have immediate access to the cash after a fire, the fund is not lent back to members but kept intact and on hand in the bank.

Run at this level of simplicity, insurance clubs have a reasonable chance of working well. Their essential characteristic is that the fund is released when – and only when – an identified contingency arises. This singularity of purpose adds discipline to the club and helps them overcome the risks of holding money for an indefinite term.[4]

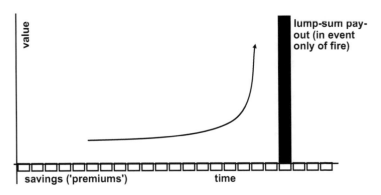

Figure 3.1 Fire insurance association

The ROSCA

The ROSCA is the world's most efficient and cheapest finan-
cial intermediary device. The best form of ROSCA, the auc-
tion ROSCA, matches savers perfectly with borrowers, and
rewards both of them.

With its description of Mary's savings club or 'merry-go-
round' Chapter Two provided an example of how the poor
can and do get together to manage their own basic personal financial intermediation. The merry-go-round is just one
of many variations of the ROSCA, the rotating saving and
credit association. ROSCAs are found in various forms on
every continent, and have been in existence for centuries.
There are references to ROSCAs in Japan dating back six
hundred years, before modern banking evolved in Europe
(Izumida 1992).[5] This essay is not about the history of the
ROSCA, nor will it offer evidence about the huge numbers
of ROSCAs found round the world: the endnotes provide
help to locate documentation that is available on those aspects of the ROSCA. Rather, having noted that the ROSCA
is an extremely popular intermediation device, we will try
to honour it by describing as simply as possible its major
variants and explaining their differences.

Anthropologist Shirley Ardener devised what has become
the standard definition of a ROSCA (Ardener 1964)[6]: 'An
association formed upon a core of participants who make
regular contributions to a fund which is given, in whole or
in part, to each contributor in rotation.'

Thus, in Mary's merry-go-round, there are fifteen members (the 'core of participants') each of whom makes a daily
contribution of 100 shillings. That daily total (1,500 shillings) is given in whole to each contributor in turn. The
process takes fifteen days. In what follows, I use the word
'round' to refer to each distribution of the lump sum (the
total number of which will equal the number of members).
The word 'cycle' is used for the complete set of rounds, after which the ROSCA comes naturally to an end (though it

may be repeated, with or without variations in the number of members, or in the amount and frequency of the contributions). In Mary's case there is a *round* each day for a fifteen-day *cycle*, and then they start another cycle.

The ROSCA's Advantages

The elegance, simplicity and neatness of the ROSCA give it great appeal, and like many others I'm drawn to it partly for that reason. I joined a ROSCA in Mexico in 1974[7] and have been fascinated by them ever since.

The virtues of ROSCAs are apparent in Mary's club, which neatly arranges the small daily savings of fifteen people into a series of fifteen large lump sums, which each member in turn enjoys. The ROSCA, which then ends (only to be reborn into another cycle), has no running costs and is wonderfully transparent – without elaborate books its accounts are clear to each and every member, even if they include the illiterate. No outsiders are involved, no one is beholden to anyone else, and no one has profited from anyone else's difficulties. Moreover, no money has had to be stored by the managers of the ROSCA, because all cash passes from member to member directly. This has two healthy results. Firstly, it greatly reduces the risk of misappropriation. Secondly, it makes ROSCAs extremely *efficient*. Indeed, ROSCAs could reasonably claim to be the most efficient intermediation device around, since at each round the savings of many are transformed instantaneously, with no middlemen and no transaction costs, into a lump sum for one person.

Perceived disadvantages

However, when people first hear about ROSCAs they often react by listing their disadvantages, as they see them. Usually, their first objection is 'what stops those who get the lump sums first from running away?' The next is 'but the system is unfair: the ones who get the lump sum first have a huge advantage. They get an interest-free loan at their fellow-members' expense'.

We have already hinted at the answers to these two objections, in the first two chapters. Many people *like* to save regularly if they can, to build up lump sums, so even the 'end-takers' still benefit from a ROSCA compared to paying a deposit-collector like Jyothi. And people tend not to run away from services that they like. However, we shall be able to build even better answers to these objections by looking at the ROSCA in more detail.

We start by listing the four main ways in which ROSCA users decide the order in which the lump sum is taken. They are by:

1. *prior agreement*
2. *agreement at each round*
3. *lottery*
4. *bidding for the lump sum*

Ways of running ROSCAs: prior agreement

Mary's merry-go-round is a ROSCA that decides the order in which the lump sums is taken by prior agreement. This type is particularly appropriate when the intention is to run many cycles of the ROSCA one after the other. After a few cycles, any 'unfairness' in the order has shrunk to insignificance, and each member's situation is the same: she gets her lump sum every fifteenth day (for example). This pattern of prior-agreement multi-cycle ROSCAs is the dominant form of ROSCA in Nairobi's slums. It provides slum-dwellers with a secure way of saving regularly and continuously. Its simplicity – no decisions about the order of disbursement apart from the initial one need be taken, and no mechanisms like lotteries or auctions are required – suits this continuous, routine savings function especially well. It means that members do not have to get together in a meeting each time the lump sum is taken, and many such

ROSCAs run without meetings, or hold meetings only at the close of each cycle (which may also be the start of the next). This makes this form of ROSCA very convenient.

Ways of running ROSCAs: agreement at each round

If members are well acquainted with one another ROSCAs can function as the second type, deciding who gets the lump sum at each successive meeting. This is usually done on the basis of who needs it the most. There are probably fewer of this kind of ROSCA than any other kind, perhaps because of the difficulties of assessing 'need' without recourse to the price mechanism (see auction ROSCAs below), and the risk that the more articulate or the more cunning will manipulate the process.

But there is a variant of this type that is quite common, in which the ROSCA is initiated by someone who suddenly needs a lump sum and who gets friends to join in. In the mountainous north of The Philippines I met rural schoolteachers who go for many months without running a ROSCA, until one of them wants cash to furnish a new home, say, and calls on her fellow teachers to start a ROSCA, usually funded from their monthly salaries. She takes the first lump sum, and accepts responsibility for the management of subsequent rounds until the ROSCA finishes.[8] Some lottery and auction ROSCAs (see below) are likewise started by an individual with a pressing need.

Ways of running ROSCAs: lottery

'Lottery' ROSCAs are a huge and varied class of ROSCA found almost everywhere. In some countries they dominate: Bangladesh is an example. The lottery avoids the problems of any perceived 'unfairness' in the order in which the lump sum is taken, or the embarrassment of comparing people's needs, by leaving the order to chance. Typically, names are drawn out of hats (or the local equivalent). Every member's name goes into the hat in the first round, but winners are excluded from the lotteries of subsequent rounds. Obviously for the last round no lottery is needed, there being by then only one remaining member who hasn't yet received the lump sum.

The lottery itself may generate some excitement, which brings a crowd of onlookers which in turn helps to make the process public and fair, though this 'festival air' tends to die down after a while. And of course members sometimes find ways around the arbitrariness of the lottery. Friends may agree to 'swap' (or share) their luck where one has a more pressing need than another, or one member may even 'buy' another member's lucky draw.

Precisely because lottery ROSCAs do *not* involve a group of friends deciding which of them most needs the cash, they can afford to have a more varied membership made up of people who don't know each other very well, or who are complete strangers. In Bangladesh, a typical ROSCA in the capital, Dhaka, is chaired by a small-time shopkeeper, known to everybody, and the regular lottery may take place at his or her shop. Not everyone comes to the meeting, and many members pay as and when they can, often between meetings, sometimes in instalments. The shopkeeper keeps the records of who has paid, and chases up late-payers. In the moral economy of Dhaka's slums it is not yet considered proper for such shopkeepers to see themselves as 'managers' of ROSCAs, so they don't normally charge a fee for the service, though they may bashfully accept 'tips' from members as a reward for the work. In some cases they are entitled to the first-round 'prize' without need of a lottery.

Ways of running ROSCAs: bidding for the lump sum – the auction ROSCA

By leaving the selection of 'winners' to chance, lottery ROSCAs are more flexible and less troublesome and can cater to a wider variety of people and needs than where the winner is decided round-by-round by group consensus. As we saw, however, members sometimes 'buy' a lucky draw from another member. There is an even more flexible way to cater fairly to a wide range of people and their individual needs and that is by setting up a market to decide who should take the lump sum at each round. This allocates cash to the member who most values it at the time, while compensating others by rewarding them richly for their patience. It thus benefits both those who are saving down ('borrowers') and those who are saving up ('savers'). It also elegantly arranges them in serial order with those who most need to borrow taking the lump sum at the beginning and those most content to save taking the lump sum at the end.

This is how these 'auction' (or 'bidding') ROSCAs work. Imagine a twelve-person ROSCA that meets monthly with each member contributing $10 (so there will be twelve 'rounds' and a twelve month 'cycle'). At each round $120 is available as the lump sum. At the first round those members in immediate need of cash choose to bid for the lump sum. Let us say that several members want the money and bid for it, and the one who most wants it bids $24 and wins. She then takes $96 of the lump sum ($120 minus 24), while her bid of $24 is given back, in equal shares, to each of the twelve members,[9] who walk off with $2 each (thus making a net contribution of only $8 each that month).

As the rounds proceed, the size of the winning bid tends to diminish, since there are fewer and fewer people in the auction. This is so because, as in other ROSCAs, each member takes the lump sum (less any bid discount) once only. At the last round there is no need of an auction, because there is only one member left. He gets the full $120.

The calculations for auction ROSCAs

Calculating how each member fares in such a ROSCA has caused arithmetic mayhem among the experts. I have made some simplifying assumptions for the calculations in the following three paragraphs. For those who don't want to be bothered with the arithmetic and prefer to skip it, the conclusion I reach is that both 'savers" and 'borrowers' do well. Borrowers get their loans at rates which compare well with those prevalent in the informal loan market, while savers get well rewarded, especially in comparison with a deposit taking service like Jyothi's.

Here's the arithmetic. Assume that the members who won the first four rounds each bid $24, members taking rounds five through eight each bid $12, and in the last four rounds there were no bids at all, so those members got the full $120. The bids total $144 (four times $24 plus four times $12). These bids were redistributed equally among the members, so each member got $12 back ($144 divided by 12). The total amount contributed by each member must equal 12 rounds of $10 each, which comes to $120, less the $12 from their share of the bids, for a total of $108. *Contributions* are thus the same for each and every member. But the total amount *taken out* by each member varies. For example, the first member took out $96 on the first round, while the last member took out the full $120 but had to wait until the last round.

Now, examining the last member in more detail, we see that he put in $108 over the year and then took out $120, so he earned $12 'interest' ($120 minus 108). He had on average $54 'on deposit' during that year.[10] So he earned $12 on $54, a rate of just over 22 per cent a year. Not bad.

The first member also put in $108 over the year, but, as we saw, she took out $96 on the very first day. So she 'paid' $12 in 'interest' for a loan that averaged $48 over eleven months. This is an interest rate of 24 per cent over eleven months, or about 26 per cent a year. Figure 3.2 shows the first and last members in our example, at the same scale.

My suggestion that the auction is a way of ensuring that the lump sum goes, each round, to the member who most needs it sometimes provokes strong disagreement. 'Not so', say these critics, 'as in much of the real world, the sums go

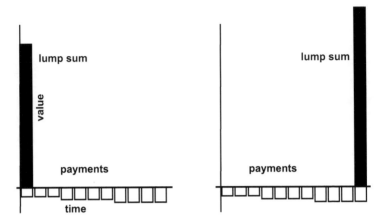

Figure 3.2 Auction ROSCA for first (left) and last (right) taker

not to those who most *need* them but merely to those who can most easily *afford* them. In this way they perpetuate the conditions that the poor unfairly suffer in so many other aspects of life'. But no matter how true that is as a general commentary on life, it isn't true in the case of an auction ROSCA. This is because even the poorest member of all can still bid in the first round, and can win it if he is willing to accept the biggest discount. He doesn't have to put extra cash on the table to win, he just has to bid the most. So he is not disadvantaged by a richer member standing next to him with his pockets bulging with cash.

The range of bid sizes in auction ROSCAs

The implied interest rates in the example above – 26 per cent a year for a loan and 22 per cent a year on savings – would, in many countries, be more attractive than most other services available to poor savers and borrowers. But these rates are not typical for ROSCAs, they are merely examples to demonstrate the arithmetic involved. In practice ROSCA members often bid much more than the modest 20 per cent of the lump sum on offer used in the example above. In northern coastal Vietnam[11] I talked to capital-hungry fishermen eager to invest in new equipment and found that in their ROSCAs, which are very common, early bids commonly reach 50 per cent of the lump sum, or more.[12] In other countries, notably India, bids are often so high that government has tried to limit them through legislation. Very high bidding means that net 'borrowers' pay a higher price for their 'loans' while those who choose to take their pay-out near the end receive very high implied rates of interest on their savings. ROSCAs are thus a very sensitive instrument for measuring, at frequent intervals, the price to the poor of capital in a local area (a point that economists and designers of financial services for the poor might note).[13]

The ROSCA 'sprint'

Sukhwinder Arora noted that in the Indian towns that we were studying many slum dwellers were pushing money through ROSCAs (particularly auction ones) at a much faster rate than through any other type of savings club or financial service. He rightly describes ROSCAs as 'sprints', comparing them to more sedate services such as a savings bank, which he calls 'marathons'. In an ordinary savings account at a bank or Post Office you might build up your savings gradually, over the long term, and it doesn't matter much if you don't save for several weeks or even months on end. In an auction ROSCA, by contrast, you commit yourself to the highest possible level and frequency of *regular* saving, by joining the ROSCA with the biggest contributions and most frequent rounds you can find (or that will let you in). For that reason the very poorest are the least well represented among users of auction ROSCAs. We noted in the first chapter that one disadvantage of devices that require fixed contributions at fixed intervals is that the very poor may be scared off or prevented from joining, because of fear of not being able to maintain the strict schedule.

As you would expect, people with businesses favour auction ROSCAs as a way of getting hold of investment capital. Equally, people with regular incomes, above all salaries, may use auction ROSCAs as a way of getting a good return on their regular savings. Businessmen can be fairly sure of being able to make the contributions at the fast pace required, and their businesses represent for them attractive opportunities for investment of the lump sum. In many societies running a business is seen as a male activity, hence auction ROSCAs are sometimes seen as 'men's ROSCAs', while lottery ROSCAs are for women. This is true, for example, in some South Asian cities.[14] Salaried people may use an auction ROSCA as a place to store their savings on a month-by-month basis, and may choose to put the lump sum, when it arrives, into a permanent home such as a savings bank. In this way they can balance the advantages of high returns and some risk (the auction ROSCA) with high security but lower returns (the savings bank).

That completes our survey of the main ROSCA types. But there are some other characteristics of ROSCAs in general that need a mention. They include the questions of trust, of innovation, and of how ROSCAs spread.

Trust, and the composition of ROSCAs

Who trusts ROSCAs enough to join them? In Dhaka, as elsewhere, there are some single-sex ROSCAs, but many are of mixed sex. Some ROSCAs are run by very homogenous groups of people – workers on the same floor of a garments factory provide a good example – but they may equally well be composed of a mixed bunch of neighbours, family and friends. We'll come back to this fact in Chapter Five when we consider Bangladesh's famous 'microfinance' banks, many of whom form groups that are very homogenous with regard to sex and class. ROSCAs, as they go on from cycle to cycle, tend to retain members who perform well, and shed ones who are difficult or slow in paying, while adding new members who are recommended by existing 'good' members. A rich mix of members of all ages and both sexes and of varying relationships results. In cases like these, where the members didn't all know each other beforehand, where does the 'trust' to run a ROSCA come from? It comes from *action*. Trust is not a commodity that can be imported automatically from some prior set of relationships. It is something that has to be made and remade, and thereby reinforced, over and over again. People stay in ROSCAs because they observe, round by round, that everyone else is obeying the rules. Trust is more of a verb than a noun.[15] Perfect strangers, coming together with the limited aim of running a ROSCA, can sometimes construct and practise trust more easily than people with histories of complex relationships with each other. But trust can be quickly broken: it is like a glass house that takes a long time to build and a moment to destroy, as the saying has it. ROSCAs can unwind quickly if the rules are breached seriously enough.

ROSCA innovation

Of course, ROSCAs can and do develop safeguards against wilful cheating. In this respect ROSCA users have proved very innovative. As far as we can tell, there were very few ROSCAs in Bangladesh until about 1980, but since then they have spread and multiplied very quickly. In so doing they have spawned many new variations. 'Rickshaw ROSCAs' are a favourite of mine. Poor men driven from villages by poverty come to Dhaka where the only work they can get is to hire a rickshaw, for say 25 taka a day, (about $0.63 in 1996, when I observed them) and hope to earn a net daily profit of, say, 80 taka (about $2). In the 1980s such men, illiterate and new to the city, and without any help from NGOs or other source, devised a ROSCA system which has worked to the advantage of many thousands of them. They group together and agree to contribute 25 taka a day to a kitty which is held, for the time being, by a trusted outsider (often the keeper of the stall where they take their tea at the day's end). Every ten days or so there is enough in the kitty to buy one new rickshaw, and that rickshaw is distributed by lottery to one of the members. The process continues until everyone has his own rickshaw. They have learnt how to arrange the number of members, the daily contribution, and the interval between rounds to best suit their cash-flow and the price of a rickshaw.

But one of their finest innovations[16] is their rule that once a member has 'won' his rickshaw in a draw, he must from then on contribute *double* each day. There is a natural justice in this, since now that he has his own rickshaw he does not have to pay to hire one, and he is therefore no worse off. It is seen as a fair way to compensate late winners for their long wait. But the device has two other effects. It shortens the length of the ROSCA cycle. This is because by the time half the members have won their rickshaws, enough extra money is coming in each day to reduce by a third the amount of time needed between rounds. And it gives winners an incentive to pay up and finish the cycle quickly, so as to hasten the day when they can enjoy the full income from each day's work. Some hard-working, single-minded men that I know came to Dhaka ten years earlier as penniless immigrants, joined successive rickshaw ROSCAs and built up big fleets of rickshaws, then sold up and bought taxis.

How ROSCAs spread – and grow

One of the curious things about ROSCAs is the distribution and incidence of the different types. For example, take South Asia. In India, in the slums and suburbs of the central city of Indore nearly all the ROSCAs that Sukhwinder Arora and I came across were of the lottery type. When we moved south and east to Vijayawada we found that most were auction ROSCAs. In Bangladesh it seems the ROSCA was virtually unknown twenty-five years ago, and today, though there are tens of thousands of lottery ROSCAs, there are still no auction ones (as far as I know), and there are far fewer ROSCAs of any type in the countryside than in the towns. In some places the ROSCA, or one particular type of ROSCA, is identified with a particular social group – a profession, maybe, or an ethnic group. Finding out how these patterns have come about is a piece of research waiting to be done. So far, we have only guesses. There is a debate going on among archaeologists about exactly how agriculture spread from the fertile plains of West Asia to Europe. Did the idea spread from village to village, by copying, or did it require the migration of a particular 'farming people'?[17] Did the lottery ROSCA arrive in Bangladesh because Bangladeshis on trips to India copied what they saw others doing, or was it brought from India to Dhaka by an immigrant group?

However they spread, there is evidence from many parts of the world that ROSCAs are enjoying a period of spectacular growth. In spite of the arrival of formal financial services they are refusing to go away. In some places they are increasing in both number and complexity.[18]

The ASCA

ASCAs are not as simple as ROSCAs, and they need more management if they are to run well. They may suffer more fraud. But their advantages are also significant: they offer the chance to use more than one type of 'swap'. Some are stable enough to arrange long-term swaps lasting several years and this advantage means that they can be adapted to work as a form of long-term insurance more easily than ROSCAs.

Wonderful though they are, ROSCAs form only one of two large classes of savings clubs.

In a basic ROSCA, a number of people meet, each puts a sum of money on the table, and then all the money is given to one person. In the minds of the members is the certainty that this simple drama will be played again next week (or tomorrow or next month) but with the money going to a different member. In subsequent rounds the scene will be replayed until everyone has taken the lump sum once. And when there have been as many rounds as there are members, it is certain that the cycle will come to an end. Then that's it. ROSCAs are *symmetrical* and *time-bound*.

But what if you start with the same basic ingredients – a group of people coming together to put cash on the table – but leave out the symmetry that, in a ROSCA, compels you to hand over the cash immediately to a fellow member? A Pandora's box of possibilities opens up. We could store the money, keeping it with the cashier or putting it in the bank. We could lend it to one of our members, or to more than one of them, or even to outsiders. If we lend it, we can, if we like, charge interest. But in that case how much interest should we charge? And how quickly should the borrower return the money? What will be the criteria for borrowing: can people take a loan for just anything, or are we all saving for a single purpose? Besides, is it even necessary to save the same amount each week? Why can't you and I save different amounts from each other, or different amounts from week to week? Do we need to save any longer once we have built up a decent fund? And anyway, how long is this thing going to go on for: a year, three years, until we have enough for us all to buy a motorbike, until some contingency arises, or forever? And who's going to keep the accounts?

Put together any combination of this long list of variables and the chances are that somewhere in the world there's an ASCA that runs like that. Out of this huge set of possible ASCA types, this chapter will describe only a handful. Interspersed among these descriptions will be a discussion of two of the biggest issues that confront any group of people who decide to set up an ASCA – *interest rates* and *longevity* (how long a life the ASCA should have).

Time-bound ASCAs

We saw an example of a time-bound ASCA when we looked at Rabeya's 'fund' in Chapter Two. In this type of ASCA, members agree to a high level of standardization and discipline. Everybody saves on the same day each week, and everybody either saves ten taka or a multiple of ten taka. For accounting purposes, the Chairperson can think in terms of ten taka units, or 'shares', of which some members have only one while others have several: this is a useful device which simplifies the book-keeping task. The life of the ASCA is set, right at the beginning, at 52 weeks, and this is rigidly respected. Loans all carry the same interest rate, loans to outsiders are not permitted (since that is seen as too risky) and all loans have to be 'in' (fully repaid) by the end of the year. Despite a certain inflexibility that these rules impose, in Dhaka ASCAs of this sort are beginning to displace ones with laxer rules. Why should this be?

In a time-bound ASCA there comes a time when the books must be closed and all the money finally and fully accounted for. This gives the ASCA something of the clarity and strength of the ROSCA, since the members either get their savings back (with profits) or they do not. ROSCAs have come to Dhaka quite recently, and are growing rapidly. Dhaka's ASCA users have seen for themselves the advantages of ROSCA-type discipline. These days ASCAs that don't meet this ROSCA-like basic test – getting your money back – die quickly. An evolutionary shuffling process sets in whereby good Chairpersons (or committees) with sound books, like Rabeya, run ASCA after ASCA, and less skilled (or even fraudulently inclined) Chairs do not get a second chance to muddle or cheat their members.

ASCAs that are not time-bound

Muddling and cheating certainly goes on. There are some parts of the world – rural Bangladesh, for example – where better-off and more articulate villagers often cheat their poorer, less-educated neighbours, intentionally or inadvertently, through the use of loosely organized and poorly run ASCAs. Responding to the need of the poor to find a place to save, they act as treasurers, and collect savings over a period of time. But in some strange way those savings disappear, or for some unexplained reason never seem to be available to the poor families that deposited them. Such unsatisfactory examples of ASCAs are usually not time-bound: there is no specified moment when the members, without embarrassment, can get an 'action audit' and can make up their own minds about how well the ASCA is running. In villages I have studied in Bangladesh (where the ROSCA is yet to penetrate the countryside), ASCAs of this sort spring up every now and again, fail, and then after an interval, so pressing is the need to save, another one starts up, only to suffer the same sad fate. It is partly for this reason that, as we shall see in Chapter Five, rural Bangladeshis so gladly accepted the much more reliable services offered to them by the Grameen Bank and its imitators.

Still, ASCAs that are not time-bound have their own virtues, the greatest of which is that they allow savings to be built up over the long term. Although ROSCAs (like Mary's) and time-bound ASCAs (like Rabeya's) can repeat themselves cycle after cycle, each cycle is complete in itself, and all the money has to be returned to the members. But as we saw in our analysis of financial services needs in the first chapter, poor people also need to save up over the long term for old age, for their heirs, for marriage, and for emergencies that may occur at any time.[19] Because, as we have already noted, it is very hard for a group of poor people to keep cash safe over the long term, most successful long-term ASCAs are managed for them by others, and we shall be looking at them in the next chapter.

Nevertheless, there are some examples of successful long-term, owner-managed clubs. Among saving-up clubs, there are the fire-insurance societies described at the start of this chapter. We noted that one reason for their success is that they are limited to a single well-defined use, and the same is true of some longer-term ASCAs. One case, found in several countries, is when better-off slum dwellers form savings clubs with the long-term aim of buying land on the outskirts of town and thereby escaping the slum. Regular pay-ins go into a fund that is banked until there is enough to buy a parcel of land, and the process is repeated until there is enough land for everyone. Britain's 'Building Societies' probably had their origins in similar devices more than two hundred years ago. In an example I studied in Dhaka, members of the club are not allowed to move onto the land (which is leased out meanwhile, often to local farmers) until the full amount of land has been bought, a device that helps to keep the group together for the long haul. This is very similar to the way a rickshaw ROSCA works, but because the price of land changes over time, members cannot be certain, at the outset, of how long their club will need to last, and the number and size of contributions cannot be fixed in the way that they are in a ROSCA. The leasing out to farmers also complicates their management, so I think of them as ASCA variants rather than as true ROSCAs.

ASCAs and their interest rates

ASCAs differ from saving-up clubs in offering two kinds of swap. In Rabeya's fund, an ASCA, members save up ahead of a pay-out, and may also borrow and then repay (or 'save down'). This means that ASCA members have to make decisions about interest rates, with the rate charged to borrowers determining in large part[20] the rate paid to savers. ROSCAs don't need to make such decisions, since they either ignore the issue (in merry-go-rounds and in lottery ROSCAs) or they allow rates to be set automatically by the bidding process (in auction ROSCAs). Before moving on to look at other ASCA types, it will be useful to discuss the issue of interest rates.

Well-meaning observers of savings clubs sometimes regard interest as, at best, a necessary evil. That is a mistake. Just as in ROSCAs the auction introduces a price mechanism that rewards savers and distributes cash to borrowers according to need, so in ASCAs interest rates can be used to manage rewards, prices and risk in ways that safeguard the interests of both savers and borrowers. The issue of interest rates is also important in determining the life-time of the ASCA and whether it opts to be time-bound or not.

But just how are the rates to be set? Well, Rabeya's ASCA charged 5 per cent a month for loans, which works out at an APR of about 60 per cent. That may sound high to people living in rich industrialized countries where the hope is that such high rates are a thing of the ill-managed past (although rates not so far short of this have been charged on credit-card debt, and are paid to loan-sharks by many low-income people). Why do ASCAs choose to charge these rates?

Inflation makes it hard to compare interest rates across countries. ASCAs in high inflation countries have to charge more interest on their loans, to prevent their fund (and thus their members' savings) from suffering a decline in value. But we can observe that even in countries with moderate inflation rates[21] – some South Asian and South-East Asian countries over the last thirty years, for example – ASCAs typically charge in the range of 3 to 8 per cent a month, sometimes more. When I researched 50 of Dhaka's ASCAs in early 1996, a time when Bangladesh's inflation rate was a modest 5 per cent a year, I found none that charged less than 3 per cent a month for loans, and one that charged an astonishing 20 per cent a month (admittedly, that one was not working well). But the single most common rate was 10 per cent a month: half the sample had chosen that rate. In the Bangladesh countryside, however, where opportunities to invest money profitably are far fewer than in busy Dhaka, and where loans are taken for consumption more often than for production, rates are lower, falling mostly in the 3–5 per cent a month bracket.

Interest rates on loans made by ASCAs affect the rate of growth and the absolute size of the club's funds. It is not always appreciated just how sensitive the growth of capital is to small-sounding changes in the interest rate. Consider an ASCA with 25 members who agree to save $1 a month each. Obviously, after the first meeting they will have a fund of $25, and after a year, $300 ($25 x 12 months). Now imagine that the ASCA decides to 'clear' all funds each month, by insisting that *all* the money is lent out to its members so that nothing is sitting idle or in the bank. If they decide to charge members 1 per cent a month for these loans then their fund will have grown to $317[22] (rather than $300) by the end of the first year (see table 3.1). By the end of the fifth year it will have grown to $2,042, and at the end of ten years it will stand at $5,751 (or $230 each member, for a contribution of $120 per member). Their money will almost have doubled.

However, if this club decides to settle on an interest rate at the low end of the range most commonly used by poor-world ASCAs – 3 per cent a month – it could look forward to a much faster growth rate. And if it followed the average rate found in Dhaka's clubs and charged 10 per cent a month, the ASCA will own (in theory) a mind-bogglingly large fund after ten years. In table 3.1, which sets out these results, I have left one of the cells blank, to give you a chance to guess the answer before looking it up in the endnote.

You will have noticed my cautious comment in parentheses – 'in theory' – and it may already be obvious to you why I had to include it. Arithmetic is one thing, real life another. In *reality* no club could sustain a policy of lending everything out to its members at 10 per cent a month for a period of ten years. It would mean that each and every member, at the start of the tenth year, would have to hold a loan of $325,000, and be paying interest each month of $32,500. That is obviously quite unrealistic.

Table 3.1 ASCA of 25 members saving $1 a month each and keeping all cash out on loan

Interest rate	Capital after 1 year (after contributing $300 in savings)	Capital after 5 years (after contributing $1,500 in savings)	Capital after 10 years (after contributing $3,000 in savings)
Zero	$300	$1,500	$3,000
1 per cent monthly	$317	$2,042	$5,751
3 per cent monthly	$355	$4,076	$28,092
10 per cent monthly	$535	$75,870	See endnote[23]

What then would we realistically expect to happen, as time goes by, to ASCAs that start off charging high rates of interest on loans? Six likely paths are immediately apparent. First, they might reduce the interest rate on loans as time goes by. Second, they might decrease the amount they save each month, or stop saving altogether. Third, they might store their excess cash in a bank instead of lending it out among themselves. Fourth, they could risk lending their money to outsiders, given that their own members' appetite for loans at high prices would be quickly sated. Fifth, they might persevere with their high rate of interest, give out bigger and bigger loans, run into repayment problems, and collapse. Sixth, they might just stop, after a number of years, and share out the profits. Or, of course, they may take some combination of these paths.

These outcomes are indeed what we observe in reality. I have seen examples of all six. The two most common courses that Sukhwinder Arora and I have observed are the first (reducing the interest rate charged on loans) and the last (winding the club up after some time). Of these two, winding the club up – making it time-bound, like Rabeya's fund – may be the safest. To see why, we need to review the options.

If the club chooses the first option, and voluntarily lowers its interest rate, its members can both save and borrow bigger amounts for longer periods as time goes by. That may help them use their savings and loans for rewarding investments and not just for consumption. These are clearly desirable outcomes, but the club has to overcome the many challenges that longevity brings – challenges that we list in the section on credit unions later in this chapter. One of these challenges is that lowered interest rates almost certainly means that the members are less hungry for loans than they were, so an important function of the club has already been achieved, and enthusiasm for it will wane. The same can be said of the second option, lowering the rate of savings or stopping savings altogether. This option has another snag, because if the members are not saving regularly, the repetitive actions on which trust is built become less effective.

The interest that can be earned at a bank is likely to be miserly compared to the rates the members have got used to earning on their savings through their loans to each other, so the third option – leaving their savings in the bank – is not very attractive either. Lending to outsiders at high rates of interest, the fourth option, is rarely sustainable in the long run because of the risk of loan loss, especially if the group doing it is composed of poor and not very powerful people. Collapse is to be avoided at all costs, since it jeopardizes each and every member's investment, so the fifth option is unthinkable.

So when the immediate appetite for loans is satisfied, and fewer and fewer members are willing to pay high rates of interest to borrow, many such clubs become 'time-bound' (even if they hadn't intended that at the start) and wrap up and distribute profits after a year or two.

Managing risks and rewards

These decisions are about managing risks and rewards, balancing likely gain against likely failure. All lending involves risk. We have seen a few ways in which ROSCAs reduce the risk of members running off with the pay-out before they've paid their share of subscriptions. ASCAs are more complex than ROSCAs (on average). For that reason, they generally need more paperwork, and better monitoring of members. But also, for that reason, there is a bigger range of ways in which risk can be managed.

In an ASCA, fresh money (as opposed to repayments of loans) comes in from two sources: the members' regular savings, and the interest they pay on any loans they take.[24] Setting interest rates adjusts the proportion of new funds that come in from these two sources. Low interest rates on loans will mean that most fresh money comes from savings, whereas high interest rates will tilt the balance so that a bigger and *growing* proportion of fresh money is coming from interest paid on loans. Table 3.1 shows this quite clearly. At zero interest rates, all the fresh money comes from savings, whereas at 10 per cent a month current income from interest payments exceeds that from savings after little more than a year.

Thus, where interest rates are high, a bigger and growing proportion of loans will be sourced from the interest payments of the borrowers themselves, and less and less from those who save but choose not to borrow. This means that if an ASCA is composed, as many are, of people who want to borrow and others who are content to save, adopting a high interest rate policy will ensure that the borrowers largely finance their own loans. In the event that something goes wrong, savers may lose their hoped-for profits but they have less capital at risk. This can be useful sometimes, as the following story shows.

Initial-investment ASCAs

In the hills of northern Philippines, as elsewhere in the country, the government encouraged user-owned financial services in the form of village-level co-operatives. Unfortunately, these were not always well conceived or run,[25] and in some places have had the result of undermining faith in all savings-based devices. People became reluctant to trust their savings to ASCAs and other forms of savings club. But the user-owned tradition is hard to kill off, and another form of ASCA has evolved. In this, members make only one initial investment, which is often quite small. The funds formed by these investments are lent out at a *very* high rate of interest (up to 10 or even 15 per cent a month) to the member(s) most in need of cash. As those borrowers, and successive borrowers, repay their loans with interest, the fund grows quickly, and that growth is financed entirely from interest payments contributed by the borrowers. Those who contribute their initial investment but do not borrow then watch their investment grow quickly, aware that this rapid growth comes at a rather high risk of failure but comforted by the thought that even total collapse will lose them only their relatively small initial contribution. In one ASCA that I looked at, they had tried to contain that risk by insisting that the club close down and distribute profits after three years. Even after so short a time, at 15 per cent a month, a saver who put in only an initial $1 could see her share of the capital multiply 133 times. Figure 3.3

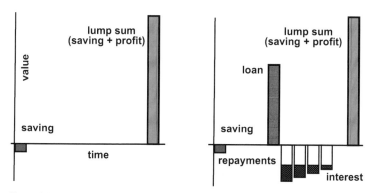

Figure 3.3 Initial Investment ASCA for the saver (left) and the borrower (right)

shows the cash flows for a net saver and the likely picture for a borrower in such a scheme.

The example shows that the collapse of confidence in 'saving up' (saving ahead of a lump sum) meant merely that people stopped saving up. It didn't mean that the *need* to save, which as we saw in the first chapter is unavoidable for the poor, had gone away. If people were no longer able to find places to store and grow savings until they accumulated into a usefully large lump sum, then they had to find some other way of swapping savings for lump sums. (Some other way, as I would say, of getting access to basic personal financial intermediation). This other way turned out to be the initial-investment ASCA, a device that reduces the need to 'save up' to the barest minimum, but forces members to 'save down' at very high rates after getting hold of their lump sums.[26]

Multiplication, reiteration, growth and permanence

ROSCAs and ASCAs offer hope and service to millions world-wide. But, we have discovered, not many of them are *permanent* institutions. All ROSCAs and, it turns out, many ASCAs, are time-bound, or end up with shorter lives than their members may have expected. Given that many modern writers on financial services for the poor are very concerned with the 'sustainability' of financial institutions for the poor,[27] it is worth pondering this fact. Let us do that now, before moving on to look at the credit union, a kind of ASCA that does aim at permanence.

We could say that the unconscious 'strategy' favoured by user-owned clubs to reach out to millions of people is 'reach lots of people through *multiplication*, and serve them continuously through *reiteration*'. Millions of individual clubs (ROSCAs and ASCAs) are constantly springing up, closing down, or restarting. Formal institutions, such as banks, are quite different: they aim to serve millions by adopting, consciously, a strategy which might be described as 'reach lots of people through *growth* and serve them continuously through *permanence*'.

We shall return to this point in Chapter Five, when we look at the differences between the new wave of 'promoters' and 'providers'. But for now we shall raise the question, 'is it possible to have long-term or even permanent *user-owned* savings clubs?'

The credit union, a permanent ASCA

Yes, it is possible, but it is not easy. And if you're poor, it's least easy of all, for reasons not so different from those used in Chapter One to explain why poor people find it hard to save at home. As time goes on, and your collective fund builds up, all the difficulties that confront you in running an ASCA have the unfortunate habit of getting more acute. More and more accountancy skills are needed. As the stakes rise (with more money in the pot) the members are more and more likely to quarrel over the rules and over book-keeping errors. As immediate borrowing needs are met, members are less likely to take all the available cash out on loan and more cash has to be stored. This is itself risky: if it's left with the cashier she might abuse it. If it's put in the bank, that means more book-keeping, more work and lower interest earnings. As others in the slum or the village learn that your fund has now grown into a substantial sum it attracts more attention and thus becomes more vulnerable to theft or to more subtle attempts to get a share of it. No wonder a common response to these conditions is to say, 'OK, let's divide the money before things go wrong, and those of us who want to carry on can get together and start a new one'.

Yet there *are* examples of successful savings clubs that remain owned by their users, have a long life and become permanent institutions. They are all in one way or other members of a group of ASCAs called variously 'credit unions' (CUs) or 'savings and credit co-operatives' or 'thrift and loan co-operatives'. To become permanent, such clubs require to be linked to a higher body that solves the set of problems set out in the previous paragraph. These higher bodies *supervise* and *regulate* the CUs, ensuring compliance with a clear set of rules. They offer CUs *financial services* that solve the problem of how and where to store surplus savings funds: this is often done in the context of an 'inter-lending' function that transfers cash from (usually older) cash-rich CUs to (usually younger) cash-needy ones. They may also offer insurance, especially insurance which relieves the heirs of members of any debt arising from a loan that is outstanding at death. Finally, they offer CUs *legal* registration, protection and representation and are able to lobby on their behalf with the authorities.

Because this set of tasks requires skills that demand education, fully fledged systems of credit unions have rarely been owned exclusively by the poor. The poor have more often been members of CUs run by the educated middle classes. Fortunately, a number of CU higher bodies around the world are now taking a fresh look at how they can better serve poorer groups. My rather brief description of credit unions can be supplemented with the literature that these bodies produce.[28]

With their several 'levels', with formal registration and supervision by registries set up by governments, with permanent salaried staffs administering interlending and insurance schemes, and with links with formal banks, credit unions are clearly very different from neighbourhood schemes like Rabeya's 'fund'. In many ways they more resemble the 'managers' that we're going to look at in the next chapter, but they belong in this section, with the AS-CAs, because, essentially, they remain user-owned savings clubs: entities that manage their own affairs as opposed to organizations that manage clubs for others.

Savings clubs and insurance

When we looked at the fire insurance ASCAs in Dhaka's slums early in this chapter, we saw how a simply structured owner-managed club can help people anticipate and cope with emergencies. But are those clubs really offering 'insurance'?

There are two ways in which financial services can offer protection against the risk of losses caused by accidents, ill-health, emergencies, theft and so on. One way is through savings and loans: that is, by providing a home for savings over the long term and by offering loans. In this case, people are helped to create a store of savings (on the one hand) and to secure rights to loans (on the other) both of which can be drawn on when needed. The approach usually depends on intermediation, using the savings of some people to provide loans for others, but each individual saver and borrower creates a lump sum that is proportional to what she puts in: savers get back a little more than they saved, and borrowers pay back a little more than they borrowed. Such intermediation is *reciprocal*.

There is also a *non-reciprocal* form of intermediation. This occurs when the device of *pooling* is used. In this case, deposits are taken from many people, but a lump sum is returned only to those who suffer a loss. The advantage of pooling, of course, is that the lump sums can be much bigger than what an individual could ever hope to save or repay in a lifetime, and are therefore more likely to be able to compensate clients for the whole of, rather than a part of, the loss they have suffered. Both systems can be described as 'insurance', but it is the second method, the pooling of the deposits of many to compensate the losses of a few, that characterizes the modern formal insurance industry.

Informal devices rarely use this non-reciprocal 'pooling' principle. Jean-Philippe Platteau (1997), has suggested that traditional communities dislike pooling because they believe that all financial transactions should be based on 'balanced reciprocity', the idea that individuals get back more or less what they are willing to put in. They believe that it is inherently wrong that some people should benefit disproportionately from the contributions of others. Perhaps that is why I have found very few examples of true pooling among informal devices, and I describe only one in this book, the 'burial fund', found in the next chapter. Among the owner-managed devices which are the subject of this chapter there are no examples of true pooling, so arguably there are no examples of 'true user-owned insurance'.

Postscript: The *ubbu-tungngul*

The chapter finishes with a curiosity. As I warned earlier, some financial services devices are hard to classify. The *ubbu-tungngul* (the 'pull-push') of northern Philippines is an example.[29] Though it has many characteristics in common with the ROSCA it is not a true ROSCA because contributions vary across members and across time. I was excited when I found my first *ubbu-tungngul*, in the mid-1990s, thinking I had discovered a unique device. But in 2005 Daryl Collins[30] showed me a version of the South African 'stokvel' (the name that describes a variety of South African ROSCAs and ASCAs) which operates in exactly the same way, on the opposite side of the world.

In the first chapter we mentioned that 'reciprocal' lending between neighbours is perhaps the most common form of informal financial transaction between poor people. I borrow a few cents from you today and on some other day you borrow a similar amount from me. If we wished we could do this on a regular basis: on the first day of each month I might borrow from you whatever loose cash you had on you that day, and on the fifteenth of each month you could borrow from me whatever I had available that day. But that doesn't sound very useful, does it?

Still, suppose I had a similar one-to-one relationship with many people, not just with you. I could agree with all of them that on a certain day they all lend me some cash, in different amounts depending on what they could afford. That would be useful, because the combined amount would amount to something substantial: it would be a 'usefully large lump sum'. Then I promise to pay them back, one by one, at fifteen day intervals. If there were ten of us then after five months I would have paid them all back and fifteen days later it would again be my turn to receive.

If you've followed my explanation so far, you'll be able to see that each of the ten of us could in turn, at five month intervals, be the 'receiver', in this case, of nine small varied amounts that add up to a large amount. On all other occasions each would be a 'payer', giving a small amount to just one of the other nine.

What would thus emerge looks superficially like a ROSCA but is more flexible, in that it allows me to vary my payments according to what I have available each 'round'. Of course, I have an incentive to put in as much as I can, so as to receive as much as I can when it's my turn. Keen *ubbu-tungngul*ers might argue that this flexibility has the effect of raising the total amount transacted, since people don't have to limit themselves to putting in only what they are sure of being able to afford each and every round. The *ubbu-tungngul* shares this virtue with *Safe*Save.

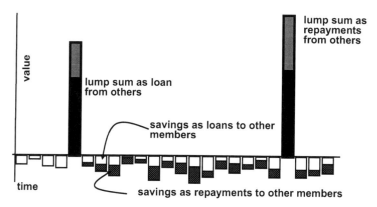

Figure 3.4 The *ubbu-tungngul*

Figure 3.4 shows the *ubbu-tungngul* from the point of view of an individual member. Each member is conducting a set of private deals with each of the other members, so why bother to go to the trouble of doing it in public at a regular meeting? Well, in part, precisely because it *is* public and regular. Concluding deals in public provides a public record of the deal, which can be useful if a dispute occurs. Doing it regularly provides that *discipline* which, as we have seen, is very important to maximize savings, especially if the amounts saved are not fixed. The conclusion of several deals on the same day with a variety of partners also ensures something else: that the biggest possible 'usefully large sum' can be assembled at one time.

So we are back where we started. Financial services for the poor are ways of helping the poor to enjoy the *discipline* and *opportunity* to *maximize* their savings and turn them into usefully *large* lump sums.

Conclusion

This chapter has looked at how poor people form clubs designed specifically to meet their basic personal financial intermediation needs: their need to turn their meagre savings into usefully large lump sums of money. It is possible that these clubs, which are found on every continent and have been for centuries, constitute the biggest family of associations of any kind (not just financial associations) among the poor. I say this because I have been in many villages and slums where savings clubs have either been the only, or the most common, type of poor-owned association. The trust that is needed to run such clubs comes from each member's repeated opportunity to observe whether her fellow members are respecting the rules: this enables clubs to take in as members people who may not know each other well.

All these clubs use one basic ingredient: saving small sums over time. They are the basis of financial services for the poor. ROSCAs collect and redistribute those savings in a regular symmetrical way (the 'saving through' way), so that every member gets treated the same. ASCAs, the other large category of such clubs, are more flexible, and build a wealth of savings which different members can use in different ways, to save up, to save down, or both.

The more sophisticated versions of both ROSCAs and ASCAs use pricing methods that help manage risk and make the device more flexible and fair. The auction ROSCA elegantly and automatically allows the price to be set by the users each time a sum is distributed, and that price can vary over time. ASCAs have to deliberately 'set' their price, which they do by means of agreeing to an interest rate. In both cases, the best devices offer good terms to borrowers (saving down) and reward savers (saving-up).

For good reasons, many savings clubs are time-bound. They still serve millions of poor people, by their unconscious strategy of 'multiplication and reiteration', a strategy that marks them off sharply from institutions like banks that aim at 'permanence and growth'. Nevertheless, if certain precautions can be taken, savings clubs can become permanent institutions, as successful credit unions have shown.

CHAPTER 4
Informal services: managers and providers

*Some organizations manage savings clubs for other people.
They often do it rather well, and are able to manage longer-
term 'swaps' than simple user-owned clubs like ROSCAs and
ASCAs. There are also many informal financial service providers, such as deposit collectors, pawnbrokers, and moneylenders,
who deal mostly with individual clients and charge for their
services.*

In the previous chapter we looked at that part of the informal sector in which groups of poor people organize financial services for themselves by running savings clubs. This
chapter is also about the informal sector and deals with
those informal services that are used by the poor but run
for them by others.

There are two kinds of people or organizations in the informal sector that run services for poor people. I call them
the 'managers' and the 'providers'. The managers include
non-profit organizations such as churches, temples, youth or
women's clubs, or trade associations, that are stable enough
to run simple savings and loan clubs for their members.
Then there are commercial managers that run ROSCAs for
other people and earn a fee for doing so. The providers, by
contrast, are people who offer unregistered financial services
to the poor for sale: typically they are moneylenders or deposit collectors of the sort we looked at in Chapter Two. As
usual, these definitions are not watertight: as we shall see,
some moneylenders lend more out of social obligation (or
even as a way to save) than out of a desire to make profits.

The chapter deals first with the managers and then with the providers.

The managers

Permanent organizations whose main business does not involve providing financial services may nevertheless manage savings clubs on behalf of their members. Their status may allow them to do this rather well. Some commercial operators specialize in running ROSCAs for the general public.

I am using the term 'managers' to describe organizations that are not themselves savings clubs, but manage clubs for others. We start with welfare-oriented organizations that manage ASCAs, and end with commercial outfits that run ROSCAs. Many of the examples come from South Asia, one from Britain, and another from Africa: but there are examples to be found on all continents.

The very simplest kinds of managed clubs are there to protect the money put into 'saving up' clubs. When I was growing up in London after the war our local grocer had a 'Christmas box' that stood on his counter alongside collection boxes for a guide-dogs charity and the life-boats association. Customers would drop coins into these boxes, and when something went into the 'Christmas box' the grocer would make a note in an old-fashioned ledger and issue a little printed ticket. He was 'managing' a saving-up club for his customers. He didn't charge directly for his management services, but he expected that customers would spend at least some of their Christmas box money in his shop, and he probably used the money in his own business during the year. Most readers will be familiar with such things, so let us move on to more complex schemes.

Managed 'funds' – the annual savings clubs of Kochi

In the city of Kochi (formally Cochin), in the southern Indian state of Kerala, you will find many slum-dwellers enrolled in clubs that closely resemble Rabeya's fund ASCA. They save set sums on a weekly basis (multiples of ten rupees) and do so for exactly a year. They may, if they wish, take a loan from the fund as it builds up, and many do. These loans are priced at 4 per cent a month and must be repaid before the year end. We don't need to make a fresh diagram since it would look exactly the same as the one we drew for Rabeya in Chapter Two.

The difference is that the Kochi's ASCAs (which are called, confusingly, Annual Savings Clubs, or ASCs) are not owned and run by their users in the way that Rabeya and her fellow members own and manage their fund. Instead, they are owned and run by temples, mosques, churches, trades organizations, and the like, who establish and run them on behalf of their congregations and constituents (Arora and Rutherford 1997).

Compared to Rabeya's members, people who use these ASCs have less control over them. They cannot easily vary the interest rate, and they have little influence over the membership. But there are important compensations for this. For one thing, the management tasks, including the vital tasks of keeping the accounts straight and chasing up non-payers, are done by others – parish or temple priests or welfare association officers doing it as part of their duties, though they are sometimes backed up by permanent paid staff. For another, the process of 'institutionalization' that we noted at work in Dhaka – the tendency for rates to become standardized – reaches spectacular heights in Kochi. In every slum that Sukhwinder Arora and I visited in that city, the rates were the same. You got 600 rupees back for each ten-rupees-per-week saved over a year, and loans cost 4 per cent a month.

Permanent welfare organizations that manage ASCAs for other people confer another advantage. We saw in the previous chapter that there are many good reasons for most true user-owned ASCAs and ROSCAs to have a short life. This makes it hard for their members to save up for long-term needs. When they do try to serve such needs they are often forced to offer a very simple service, as we saw in the case of the fire insurance societies of Dhaka, which cannot lend their fund out because they need it to hand in case there's a fire. 'Managers', on the other hand, as a result of their greater size and permanence, are much better placed to serve longer-term needs.

Managing long-term needs – the 'marriage fund'

I have in my collection a simple passbook printed in the rounded text of Malayalam, the language of Kerala. It is issued by a local fisherfolk's 'Development Welfare Co-operative Society' just outside Kochi, and is for their 'Sadhbhavana Marriage Aid fund'. The first few pages set out the rules with admirable clarity.[1]

The unmarried men, women and children of the fishing community can join the scheme, or have relatives join in their name. In practice, parents and grandparents commonly take out membership in the names of their infants. They choose a fixed regular payment – let us say the equivalent of $1 each week – and start saving. These savings build up and are released back to the saver (or the saver's nominee) when he or she marries, along with a dividend worth exactly the amount saved to date (providing that at least three years have gone by). In the meantime, if the savers need access to their savings for some reason, they can take and repay a loan from the fund that is building up.

Such schemes provide savers with a place to store savings over the long term, guarantee them a lump sum to get back at a time when they're sure to need it, and provide them with a bonus too. Over and above this they offer their members the chance to take a loan when they need it. Figure 4.1 is drawn to show how one saver might use such a club. I have assumed that he (or she) joined the club at the age of nine and married at 17, and took two loans during that time.

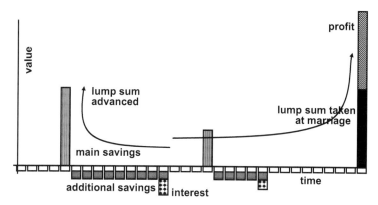

Figure 4.1 The marriage fund

How can the society be so generous? After all, if I join and save $100 and get married after three years, they will have to pay me $100 as a dividend. That's an interest rate of 67 per cent a year![2] But of course very few people marry three years after joining the club. Do the arithmetic again assuming that the *average* marriage takes place nine years after joining the scheme. The saver still gets double what he put in, and of course he's put in much more, so the bonus is now a huge $300. The saver is happy even though the *rate* at which he has earned interest has come down to just over 22 per cent a year. That is less than 2 per cent a month. So if the society lends out the savings funds at 4 per cent a month (as it does) it has a good 'margin' to cover its costs and any losses, even if it doesn't lend out the whole of its fund all the time.

What about those who do not get married? Well, the society has a rule that at 35 years of age you can take back your savings even if you remain single. So if you started saving aged 9, by 35 you'll get a big pay-out, no doubt, but the society will have paid you interest at less than 8 per cent a year.

Managing insurance needs: burial funds

In a marriage fund, you save up for an event that is very likely to happen, and you don't get your money back until that event happens (or you get to be 35). In other words, the pay-out is contingent on a named event, and the fund is clearly offering a kind of insurance, even though what you get back is what you put in plus interest earned on it: this is not true 'pooled' insurance. Managed ASCAs can address these insurance needs more successfully than user-owned ones.

Alongside its marriage funds the Kochi-based fisherfolk's co-operative societies offer 'burial funds'. These are even more obviously an insurance device. Some are time-bound and some are not. The non time-bound version works similarly to the marriage fund, with a fund that grows over time and with loan entitlements attached. The time-bound version, however, is different. It uses 'pooling', and is therefore a 'true' insurance scheme. It works as follows.

As a member of an *annual* burial fund, I agree to pay a fixed sum each week for a year. If anyone in my family dies during the year, the next-of-kin gets an immediate no-questions-asked pay-out, which is also a fixed amount. At the end of the year the books are closed. If the total weekly payments collected have exceeded the total pay-outs (which is normally the case) then the balance is re-distributed back to the members. If the total is less than the pay-out, members are asked to share the cost of making up the deficit.

When Sukhwinder Arora and I investigated these burial funds, we found that the managers made sure that each fund had at least 300 subscribers. With a smaller number, the fund was prone to run out of cash if there was an above-average number of deaths in the first few weeks. Given that one subscription covered everyone in the family ('the member, his wife, husband, father, mother, unmarried children, unmarried brother and sister, dependants, etc.', it says in the Sadhbhavana rules) we were puzzled as to how the clubs could calculate the likely number of deaths (the 'actuarial' analysis). The answer was, by experience. Many churches, clubs, temples, mosques, and trade associations have run such funds over many years, and the ratios have been learnt over time. The ratio is 1:500 – for every 1 rupee contributed per week there would be a pay-out per death of 500 rupees.[3] This ratio cropped up over and over again as we went round asking about different funds: another example of what I have called 'institutionalization'.

As we have seen, the total contributions were normally found to have exceeded the total pay-outs, and this was intentional. For the managers, it is easier to give back excess cash than to collect a shortfall. And giving back cash has other healthy effects: it gives the members the impression that the club is well run, and provides them with a little cash to make their first subscription for the following year.

At that time in Kochi, the weekly pay-in for a burial fund was 2 rupees, or about 4 cents US. If that was too little for you, you simply took out two or three or more memberships (or shares). Because the minimum was set so low, we found that these burial funds reached a poorer group of clients than any other savings club or financial service in Kochi. In some poor slums it was hard to find people who weren't members of a burial fund. Fear of imposing a financial burden on the family at the time of death is very common among the elderly poor, especially widows, all over the world,[4] and this simple device much assuages that anxiety.

Figure 4.2 describes the time-bound burial club. We have shown eight years, with a death occurring during the eighth year. As in the previous diagram, for presentation simplicity the weekly payments have been shown in quarterly summaries.

Chits, or managed auction ROSCAs

Mary (in Chapter Two) ran her own merry-go-round with 14 friends. But we noticed that in Dhaka many ROSCAs

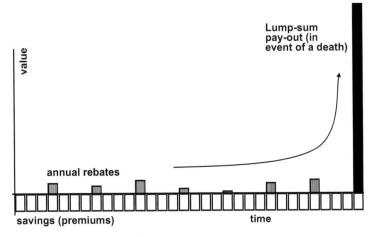

Figure 4.2 The annual burial fund

have a Chair who looks after most of the management of the club, and this is the more normal case. It is not a very long step from that to having specialists who run ROSCAs for other people on a professional fee-paid basis. It hasn't happened in Bangladesh yet (as far as I know) but it is very well established indeed in India, especially in the southern parts. Sometimes a slum-dweller or a middle-class resident will run these 'chits' (as they are known) for their neighbours on an informal but for-profit basis. But pawnbroking goldsmiths and, above all, specialist 'chit houses' run them under licence from the state governments.

They initiate the chit (the ROSCA) and take the responsibility to find the members, who may not and probably don't know each other. They then ensure that the contributions are made on time. These are all auction ROSCAs, so the company also arranges the auction at its offices. The company earns a fee from the auction winners as they take their lump sums. The company itself doesn't put up any capital: its contribution is the management skills and the willingness to take a risk, since some members may try to evade their responsibility to pay.

In the big cities, like Chennai or Hyderabad, where there are thousands of chit houses, the poor and the very poor are not the principal customers. These chits are usually 'bigger' than the poor can afford, with monthly contributions of thousands of rupees. But many middle-class Indians use commercial chits to raise a lump sum quickly, perhaps to part-finance a house purchase or a marriage. They find it easier than going to a bank.

There is even a class of professional chit 'investor': people who 'play' the chits to extract the biggest income from them. They do this by judging the best time to bid. The 'best time' will be a trade off between leaving their cash in the kitty as long as possible so that they gain the biggest prizes for the smallest bids, and taking it out quickly so as to move their money into a more profitable home. In this way chits compete with other forms of investment such as the Mumbai stock exchange, and I have been told by a chit manager that the amount of money flowing into chits can be correlated with the fluctuations of Mumbai's exchange index.

The informal providers

Some informal financial service providers offer deposit-taking: many others offer a bewildering variety of loans. All allow the poor to build usefully large lump sums out of their savings. Most providers prefer to deal with individuals, and most charge for their services, even though they are not always driven by the profit motive. In general, urban services are more professional, more precise and more disciplined than rural services.

There are many ways of providing informal financial services, and this section doesn't aim to list them all. Instead, I have classified them into four categories, and in discussing them I shall try to illustrate the particular version of basic personal financial intermediation that each of them provides. The first category is deposit collection (for 'saving up', like Jyothi's work in Chapter Two). The other three are all advances ('saving down') of one sort or another. The second category offers advances against savings, like the urban moneylender described in the first chapter. The third and fourth offer advances against assets: existing assets in the case of pawn and mortgage (category three), and future assets in the case of crop advances (category four). Table 4.1 shows them.

Deposit collectors

Jyothi's service, described in Chapter Two, illustrates the basic need for deposit collection and how that need can be met by an informal provider. We don't need to add much here. Such services are widespread, though not universal. Although our example came from India, deposit collectors appear to be much more common in Africa, above all West Africa, than in Asia, for reasons that are not well understood. Perhaps they are still on their way, and most Asians will have to wait a few more years.

In West Africa deposit collectors are found in rural as well as urban settings, and their recent growth in Nigeria demonstrates how seriously they are taken as a direct competitor to formal savings banks. There, around the turn of

Table 4.1 Four types of informal provision of financial services

Deposits	(Saving up)	
1	Deposit collection – the collection and storage of savings deposits	
Advances	(Saving down)	
2	Advances against a flow of cash deposits – a lump sum given in return for a series of small sums	
3	Advances against assets – pawnbroking and mortgaging	
4	Advance sale of produce – a lump sum repaid from the crop harvest	

Note that these are types of provision, not types of provider. Many providers offer more than one service.

the century, male bicycle-mounted daily deposit collectors known as *alajos* saw their business grow as more and more formal banks got into trouble. Soon, microfinance banks in the region started offering products based on what the *alajos* do.[5] Like Jyothi, the *alajo* uses the discipline of a set saving sum, normally in the range of 50 to 75 cents per day. His way of collecting his fee is also designed to encourage his clients to save regularly, since he charges one day's deposit per month, irrespective of how many times the client deposits. Thus, for the clients the more regularly they deposit the lower the fee as a proportion of the cash handled. But unlike Jyothi, he allows his clients to withdraw whenever they like. In this, his service is more flexible, more like *Safe*Save's. *Alajo* clients are well served: they are given a daily inducement to save, backed by a daily opportunity to withdraw. This is basic personal financial intermediation in a very pure form. Clients seem to like it: asked about the inherent risk of using a dishonest *alajo*, they are reported to have remarked that many banks – whose services are in some way inferior to the *alajo's* – can be dishonest, too.

Advances against a flow of deposits

Some *alajos* store the cash they collect in banks, while others offer cash advances to their clients. In this latter service they resemble the urban moneylender described in Chapter Two and, with him, illustrate our second category of informal provider.

The urban moneylender has his rural equivalent, though in many countries there are interesting differences, in both the services offered and the providers themselves. Here, we will look at two of these differences.

Urban moneylenders are more likely to insist on a regular periodic flow of repayments (though by no means all do so), as in the case of Ramalu's moneylender, illustrated in Chapter Two. This may be because city incomes, even for the very poor, are often small but frequent, so that clients are more able to repay advances, both from savings out of income as money flows in, and from savings out of regular expenditure as money flows out. The moneylender can tap the rickshaw driver's daily income as well as his wife's housekeeping. In the countryside this is less often the case, because incomes for small farmers are more 'lumpy' (are received in bigger sums at less frequent intervals). Rural moneylenders are therefore more willing to let borrowers repay irregularly and infrequently.

They are more able to do this because clients in many rural areas remain much less anonymous than in the cities. The moneylender in the village is more likely to know the borrower intimately, and to know his or her family. As a result, he (often she: there are many women lenders) has less need of the discipline of regular instalments to ensure that the advance gets repaid.

This leads us to the second common difference between the urban and the rural scene. Though there are many casual loans given and taken in the slums, the urban moneylender is rather more likely than his rural counterpart to be a *professional*, deriving a part, if not all, of his income from his moneylending services (Patole and Ruthven 2002). The rural equivalent is much more likely to be a part-timer. Rural moneylenders tend to be salary-earners (both active and retired-with-a-pension), traders, and middle or larger-scale farmers. Few earn the majority of their income from moneylending. Many would rather not lend money at all, but do it out of a sense of obligation. It is very hard for a moderately well-to-do villager to refuse a loan to a very poor relative or neighbour whose child has fallen ill or who has nothing to eat in the house. This does not mean that there are no rapacious rural moneylenders, of course, but they may be less common than is often supposed.

Yet another reason for lending money in the countryside is to store it. If you have excess cash and no safe place to keep it at home, then why not lend it to a trusted family member or neighbour who needs it? We saw in the description of 'saving down' in Chapter One, that many loans are, from the borrower's point of view, simply an inverted way of saving. We now see that the same can be true from the lender's point of view.[6] This ambiguity can be reflected in the words used to describe the transactions. In Bangladesh, for example, people often say that they have 'placed' money with someone else, and it can be hard to discover whether they mean they have lent the money or given it to someone else to safeguard. Sometimes those involved in such transactions prefer to keep the deal politely ambiguous, and in some cases the sum may flip, over time, from loan to savings or vice versa.

The combination of reasons for rural moneylending – out of obligation, as a way of saving, and out of a desire to profit – make up a rich, but hard to define, picture of rural moneylending which varies from country to country.

A typical rural situation is illustrated by a moneylending couple that I visited regularly in northern Vietnam for five years in the 1990s.[7] An educated couple, younger, shrewder and more ambitious than most of their neighbours, they owned and ran a shop in a small village in a remote mountainous area. Their shop had been expanding gradually and they had added other small enterprises to it. They had always lent out money, but as their own fortunes fluctuated they did so with more or less enthusiasm. Twice they told me that moneylending is a fool's game, too risky to be worth while, and that they were about to give it up. At other times they told me that their loans were doing well. They preferred to lend modest sums (not more than $300) to other prosperous villagers engaged in developing assets like fish ponds or orchards. They also lent much smaller sums, reluctantly, to the poor. In each case they lent only to those well known to them. They charged 6 per cent a month, but claimed to have taken losses on loans to both kinds of borrower. They did not have set repayment intervals, and were obliged to chase borrowers and take whatever repayments could be had at whatever time. Their transactions are part of the rural conventions. Whereas professional urban moneylenders offer an unambiguous financial service, much rural moneylending is a 'service' only in the extended sense in which we can say that petty borrowing and lending among family and neighbours constitutes a 'service'. Rural moneylending can be basic personal financial intermediation at its most diffuse.

Advances against assets

The most common forms of advance against an asset are pawnbroking in the towns and land mortgage in the countryside, though of course just about any asset can be pledged as security for a loan.

Urban pawnbrokers prefer to lend against precious metals. A typical pawnbroker in non-Muslim South Asia, for example, will work from a goldsmith's or silversmith's shop and will lend against gold, silver and brass. As a smith he will have the skill and the chemicals to test the metals for their value. He will have a different interest rate for each metal.[8] A customer taking a gold ornament to the pawnbroker will expect to receive around two-thirds the market value of the gold, and for each month he holds the loan he can expect to pay 3 per cent of the loaned amount in interest. For a loan against a silver 'pledge' he might pay 5 per cent a month, and 9 per cent for one against brass. In India, brass is a popular metal for cooking pots, so many poorer families can get a quick loan against their kitchen utensils. Perhaps for this reason some pawnbrokers now take aluminium pledges: aluminium is rapidly replacing brass as the favourite metal for cooking pots.

Speed is an important characteristic of urban pawning. Unlike advancing money against a flow of savings, an advance against a physical object requires no prior knowledge of the customer, so the deal can be struck on the spot with a stranger (though the sensible pawnbroker needs to feel confident he is not accepting stolen goods). This anonymity is another advantage of pawning, from the customer's point of view, since the neighbours don't need to know about the reason for the pawn, which might be embarrassing.

Speed and anonymity are enough to ensure that pawn-broking will remain popular, even in those countries whose governments have driven it underground by banning it.[9] But as a basic personal financial intermediation service it has snags, too. As we remarked in the first chapter, pawn-ing is of use only to those who have something to pawn, so the size of the transaction is limited by the value of as-sets the customer already holds. Moreover, unless you have a particularly friendly pawnbroker, you have to take the whole of the loaned amount back to him to get your as-set back, so to amass that sum you may need *another* basic personal financial intermediation device, such as a deposit collector or moneylender, to build up that sum from your flow of savings. If you cannot do this, you run the risk of losing the asset entirely.

When the pawnbroker takes the pledged gold ornament from his customer he does not normally *use* it: he *possesses* and stores it until the customer reclaims it or until it is clear that the customer isn't going to reclaim it. In that event the pawnbroker sells it or melts it down and uses it as raw material in his smithy. In the countryside, when land or assets are given as security (a 'mortgage') for a loan, there are various combinations of use and possession. Sometimes merely an 'interest' in land is 'conveyed' to the mortgagee (the creditor), while the mortgagor (the landowner who be-comes the debtor) continues to use it, just as a house-buyer in the west lives in the house he has mortgaged to the com-pany that gave him a loan to buy the house. More com-monly, the mortgagee takes over and uses the land, though he might choose instead to claim a share of its produce. If the asset is not land but, for example, a tree, or even a cow, the fruits of the tree or the young or milk of the cow may belong to the mortgagee for the duration of the deal. The variations are endless.

From the point of view of poor mortgagors, land mortgage suffers from similar drawbacks to pawning: it is limited by the value of the assets already in their possession, and carries the risk of losing the assets forever. It is difficult to amass the sum of money required to redeem the asset, and simple devices to help the poor do this (such as those provided by deposit collectors or cash moneylenders) are in short supply in the villages, as we have seen. Then again, because of the legal procedures involved, the deal can take a long time to conclude, and the illiterate poor are put at a particular disadvantage and can be cheated. As with advances against savings, conditions for advances against assets are generally less accessible to the rural than to the urban poor, and the devices available are less precise, less quick, and less reliable.

Nevertheless, asset mortgage is commonly practised in many villages world-wide, suggesting that the supply of more convenient financial services remains inadequate. Despite this, it is not always the case that the poor are mortgagors dealing with exploitative wealthy mortgagees, as the example of the *kat* deal in Bangladesh reveals. A *kat* is an open-ended land mortgage in which the mortgagee, in return for a lump sum, enjoys the use of the land until and unless the mortgagor returns the sum in full. It is often used by middle-income rural families to get out of farming and into some off-farm business – perhaps a small shop in the nearby town or in the capital. They raise capital by concluding *kat* agreements with a number of poorer families among whom they parcel out their land. A poor family who can raise a bit of capital, often through joining one of the new wave of microfinance providers that we shall examine in Chapter Five, can use the deal to get access to land in the long term.

Advance sale of produce

A poor farming family needing cash to get them through the growing season can, in many countries, raise money against the expected harvest. For many such families, this is the most common kind of financial transaction they get involved in. It is often common enough to have a special name and for regions to have standardized prices. In some parts of Indonesia, for example, it is called *ijon*. When I lived in southern Bangladesh I observed that for many years in the 1980s and 1990s the standard practice was for the lender to take one *mon* of paddy (about 40 kilograms[10]) for each 100 taka borrowed. Given a growing season of five months and a post-harvest market value for paddy at that time of about 200 taka per *mon*, this represented an interest rate in the order of 20 per cent a month.

In such deals the loan is not given specifically for crop input costs. The family that takes the loan *might* use it for seed and pesticide and fertiliser, but they are just as likely to use it to feed themselves while the crop is in the ground, having exhausted their reserves investing in the planting. They might also use it in some other way, such as for the life-cycle needs that we listed in the first chapter. In terms of basic personal financial intermediation these arrangements represent an extreme case. The lump sum is taken for any of the normal needs, but is matched not by a *flow* of repayments made out of savings, but by one single large act of saving made out of the family's largest single lump of income, the harvest.

The provider of the advance might be any one of the set of moneyed villagers that we listed when we looked at rural moneylenders: salaried people, pensioners, bigger farmers, traders, and so on. But he might be a paddy trader, and he might use the advance to further his business. Such arrangements can lead to long strings of lenders-and-borrowers. I looked at this phenomenon when I investigated the *dadon* system in southern Bangladesh, through which freshwater prawn production is financed.[11] There, a poor villager with a prawn pond may accept an advance against his future production of prawns from a small prawn trader who thereby extracts a promise from the borrower that he will sell all his prawns at an agreed price to the lender. That small trader may himself be indebted with similar conditions to a bigger trader in the nearby town who may be indebted to a major wholesaler at the export port where the freezing plants are located, and he in his turn may be in debt to a wealthy absentee financier with a big home in the more expensive parts of the capital.

Such systems illustrate the complexity of informal finance, and hint at its importance in national economic life. They take us away from basic personal financial intermediation, however, and will not be pursued further in this essay.

Conclusion

This chapter and the previous one have demonstrated the wide variety of ways in which the basic financial intermediation needs of poor people, who do not have access to formal services, have been met within the informal (including the 'do-it-yourself') sector.

But apart from satisfying our curiosity, how does this knowledge help us in the task of setting up more and better financial services for poor people? It helps in three main ways:

First, it shows how patchy the distribution of services available within the informal sector is. Some slum dwellers and villagers enjoy services that are quite unavailable to their counterparts in neighbouring countries, or even within the same country or district. Geographically, then, financial services for the poor still have a lot of territory to cover.

Second, it shows the extent to which informal services have been able to react to specific differentiated financial service needs. But these too are patchily distributed: in any one city or village some poor people will have access to deposit services, others to basic loan services, others to insurance services, others to several different kinds of services at once, and some to no services whatsoever. In terms of product variety, then, financial services for the poor still have a long way to go.

Thirdly, it shows that the informal sector has already reached levels of sophistication in handling technical issues such as the setting of interest rates. In many cases, this level of sophistication is well beyond anything achieved, so far, by the recent wave of new organizations aiming to provide services to the poor.

Those new organizations are themselves the subject of the next chapter.

CHAPTER 5
Welcoming new partners

Poor people now have new partners in their struggle to manage their money. First came non-governmental organizations hoping to use financial services as a vehicle for social, political and economic development. Some helped people set up savings clubs while others retailed savings and loan services directly to the poor. By the turn of the century several schemes had reached millions of poor people. Now that it has become clear that they were also highly profitable, the wider, profit-driven finance industry has taken notice, and joined in.

So far, we have seen that poor people meet their needs for financial services, if at all, in the 'informal sector', by running their own savings clubs of one sort or another, or by using local providers. Mostly, they have been left on their own to get on with it. Bankers assumed that profits couldn't be made from supplying financial services to people with such tiny means, and governments and welfare organizations sought other ways to alleviate poverty.

Still, the poor's money problems have never been entirely ignored by the wider world. There has always been concern about cruel moneylenders (think of Shylock in Shakespeare's play *The Merchant of Venice*). There have also been official worries about poor debtors. Britain's colonial administrators regularly fretted about them, and in many colonies introduced legislation against 'usury', or exploitative moneylending (McGregor 1994). After the Second World War many newly independent governments and their donors devised rural credit schemes designed not only to protect the poor from moneylenders but to help them adopt new farming techniques. Much of this effort, though, had disappointing results.[1]

But since the 1970s newer forms of 'pro-poor banking' have emerged. Most were developed by non-government organizations (NGOs) and by the 1990s there were enough of them, receiving enough attention from aid agencies and governments, to hold an international 'summit' in Washington DC to publicise their work, attract more support, share ideas, and set targets.[2] At first their work was called 'microcredit', or 'microenterprise credit', reflecting an initial focus on lending poor people money to build small businesses. Later, when a broader mix of services, including savings, were offered, the term 'microfinance' became common, and the organizations that practised it became known as 'microfinance organizations' or 'institutions' (MFOs or MFIs). Collectively, they are sometimes known as the 'semi-formal' sector of finance, to distinguish them from both the informal clubs and managers we saw in earlier chapters, and from the formal regulated banking and insurance industry. Their purpose was not to make profits but to use finance to fight poverty and promote other development goals.

The best of them soon showed that they could deliver their loans profitably and at great scale. For example, at the time of the 1997 'Microcredit Summit' Grameen Bank was serving more than two million poor borrowers in the villages of Bangladesh and covering the costs of doing so from interest charged on its loans. Their success began to attract the attention of the established finance industry, and of investors in such markets, and since the turn of the century growth has been explosive. Formal banks have partnered with or invested in 'MFOs', or have launched their own microfinance services.[3] Microfinance NGOs have transformed themselves into formal banks and some have listed on stock exchanges. Wall Street has seen microfinance as an exciting new 'asset class', and funds designed to help investors pile into it have been established and quickly subscribed (Reille and Foster 2008; Charitonenko et al. 2004). The profit motive has edged its way into microfinance and is becoming its most potent driver of growth. Microfinance is being drawn into the wider finance industry, and is becoming more focused on financial development than on social development goals.

This sketch shows that the microfinance story has grown long and complex, and it is not the job of this book to tell it (for a view of the story see Robinson 2001: see also Helms 2006). Our focus remains the money-management efforts of the poor. What does the microfinance industry look like from the point of view of poor people used to managing their finances on their own? How useful has the work of these newcomers been to them?

The Promoters

When we looked at user-owned-and-managed clubs in the third chapter we found a thriving set of self-help devices distributed unevenly across geographical areas and social groups. Would it not be a good idea to carry the idea of such clubs to poor people in places where it is not yet known, so they can set up their own clubs?

Some development NGOs and, more lately, some governments think the answer is 'yes', and they have been busy promoting savings clubs among the poor. I call them the 'promoters' to distinguish them from others who provide services directly to poor people.

Village Savings and Loan Associations

Promoters of Village Savings and Loan Associations (VSLAs) believe that a straightforward way to foster the growth of indigenous savings clubs owned and run by their members, like the ones we saw in Chapter Three, is simply to spread the message about them. Once the clubs are up and running well, the promoter can move on to the next village.

VSLAs are based on a very simple kind of time-bound indigenous ASCA found in West Africa. Members of such ASCAs make periodic savings together for a short term, often a single agricultural season. They lend out the savings among themselves, repay before the end of the term, and then take back their savings along with earnings from any interest charged on the loans. Then they can disband, or start a new cycle, then or later, as best suits their situation. We need no diagram because these clubs are a simple version of Rabeya's fund (described in Chapter Two).

For reasons explored later in this chapter, time-bound ASCAs of this sort were not usually seen as good models for would-be promoters who mostly wanted to set up *permanent* clubs. But some officers of the NGO CARE in Niger, in the early 1990s, saw virtue in precisely the feature that discouraged others – the short-term life, or 'time-boundedness'. They saw that in conditions where it would be very hard to establish permanent microfinance services, strong *im*permanent local systems based on these ASCAs could play an important role. In areas that are remote or isolated, or lack basic financial infrastructure such as banks, or have a very marked seasonal economy, or where the population is nomadic, or where literacy levels are very low, there are severe and sometimes insurmountable obstacles to setting up permanent financial services. Simple ASCAs at least give the poor in these areas an opportunity to turn their capacity to save into lump sums. Helping them to run more such clubs, and run them better, should not only help them manage their money and their lives more successfully, it was thought, but the very act of coming together to run the clubs should be good for self-confidence and community cohesion. Combining an interest in financial development with social development goals has been a common ambition of microfinance.

When they began spreading the VSLA idea, first in Africa and later elsewhere, the promoters kept the basic structure of the ASCA but added some improvements, especially by developing simple mnemonic devices[4] to help illiterate members keep better records, and by suggesting new ways to keep the funds safe between meetings (VSLA undated; and Allen and Staehle 2008). VSLAs have done well. In mid 2008 there were about a million members in VSLAs in 20 countries where they have been promoted by a growing number of NGOs and even by government-sponsored agents.[5] No-one can be sure of exactly how many VSLAs and members there are, partly because they are not permanent so that numbers wax and wane as circumstances change, and partly because NGOs move on and don't need to keep in touch with the clubs they promote – a key cost-cutting element of their strategy. Moreover, VSLAs these days are sometimes promoted by or copied from each other, as well as by NGO promoters.

VSLAs, in the simple form I have described here, handle only their own members' money. They do not borrow money from external sources such as banks. In many areas where they are found, there are no banks nearby. Nevertheless, the sharpest debate going on among VSLA promoters is precisely about whether, and under what conditions, external funds could be injected into VSLAs.[6] The question is critical. As long as VSLAs revolve only their own money they remain similar to the indigenous savings clubs we reviewed in Chapter Three. As soon as they take external funds, things become more complicated. The best place to see that is India.

Indian 'Self Help Groups'

In the1980s NGOs in India became interested in ASCAs, of which there are many in the country. They thought such clubs could be used for social, political and economic development work among the poor. The outcome was spectacular, in that their work grew eventually into the world's largest effort to promote new savings clubs. It is known as the 'Self Help Group' (SHG) movement. It grew quickly after 1992 when a government bank, the National Bank for Agriculture and Rural Development (NABARD), started promoting SHGs (as the clubs were called) and supervising and funding retail banks willing to lend to them. NABARD estimated that at the end of March 2007 more than 2.8 million SHGs had loans outstanding with banks with a total value of 123 billion Indian rupees (about $2.8 billion). Overall, 4.2 million SHGs, representing 58 million members, held savings accounts at banks.[7] For more on SHGs, see the recent overviews by Frances Sinha (2006; 2008).

The early SHGs that I visited in the 1990s[8] had many features that reminded me of indigenous clubs like 'Rabeya's fund'. They had between a dozen and twenty members, drawn from the same neighbourhood. They met regularly, sometimes weekly but more often monthly, to deposit savings. As the fund built up it was lent back to members, who repaid according to a fixed periodic instalment plan or, more rarely, in a lump sum at the end of a term. Interest was usually charged on the loans. This income could be ploughed back into the common fund, or paid to members as interest on their savings or as a 'dividend' (a share of the profits). Sometimes, to keep the funds for lending as large as possible, members were not allowed to withdraw their savings.

In other respects these NGO-promoted groups differed from truly indigenous ASCAs. There was usually an NGO officer present at the meetings, to help things along. Most SHGs were composed only of women, whereas unassisted savings clubs can be of either sex or can be mixed. Leadership of SHGs tended to be elected and to revolve annually, whereas unassisted groups often have an informal chair who is unlikely to be changed as long as he or she performs well. The average level of interest charged on loans was lower in SHGs than in unassisted groups. SHGs often had several objectives: women's empowerment, poverty reduction, leadership development, 'awareness raising' (about issues deemed to be important for the poor), business growth, or even family planning or the development of group-based businesses were advocated by NGO officers as the main work of the group, and they often insisted that some time was spent discussing these matters at each meeting. This contrasts strongly with unassisted groups who normally come together for the single unambiguous purpose of creating lump sums out of small deposits. Promoters often lent money to their SHGs or helped and encouraged them to take loans from banks, while unassisted groups rely on their own money alone. Finally, the SHGs struggled to become permanent, whereas unassisted groups find many good reasons to close their groups and start up another one.

Promoter preferences

These differences came about because the aims of most of the NGOs (and their backers, the donors) were not the same as those of most poor people who set up their own clubs. They were more complex, embracing social and political development ambitions as well as financial ones. Unassisted groups usually focus on the financial goals: they just want to turn small sums into large ones in as quick and convenient a way as possible. Promoter-NGOs had a much grander vision. They were *development* organizations, and came to SHGs from a background of social or political activism. They were not merely interested in spreading the idea of savings clubs like ASCAs and ROSCAs for their own sake. Instead they wanted to 'develop' and 'empower' the poor, and saw the savings clubs as a good way of getting the poor together to work on such ends. SHGs were described as 'entry points' for social and political development.

This helps explain the differences between NGO-promoted SHGs and unassisted clubs. Most SHGs were made up of women because the NGOs believed that women had been neglected by 'development', and they wanted to reverse this. The annually revolving leadership of SHGs came from the NGOs' interest in 'leadership development': the idea that the poor may make gains if they can train leaders who can press their case with officials and others who have influence over their lives. The lower interest rates reflected a widespread belief that interest is inherently undesirable and high rates of interest exploitative, a 'moral' view common among NGO workers in India at that time. Some had a hard time coming to grips with the power and usefulness of the judicious use of interest, and many NGOs were anxious to keep rates as low as possible. Several remarked to me that 'if the SHG members have to pay high rates of interest, they might as well stick with the moneylenders and not form a group at all'. It is for them especially that I tried to show, in Chapter Three, the importance and usefulness of a pricing mechanism in savings clubs.

Some NGOs believed that SHGs should enable members to set up and run businesses, and some thought the businesses should be jointly owned. Assuming that the members' savings would never be enough to finance businesses, they lent money to the SHGs they promoted, with funds provided by donors and, later, helped SHGs to get loans from banks. Indeed, their pioneering work in persuading the authorities and the banks that lending to SHGs is possible and should be legally facilitated, work that is sometimes forgotten now that the banks play such a big role in SHGs, was remarkable. However, NGOs may have underestimated the power of regular savings to build up capital, or misunderstood the conditions under which members would commit to such savings. A story illustrates this.

Visiting SHGs in lower-middle income areas of Indian towns I often expressed surprise at the tiny amounts the members were saving. The accompanying officer from the NGO would say 'they are very poor – they can't afford to save more than 20 rupees a month'. But after some conversation with the members it emerged that almost all of them were also members of local ROSCAs, each putting in average sums of 200 rupees a month or more.[9] When capital to create a loan can come only from savings, as in user-owned indigenous ASCAs and ROSCAs, members dig deep into their pockets to find the savings. When the capital comes from outside, for example from banks or from donors via NGOs, members, rationally, hold back their savings until the last minute when the loan just has to be repaid. That behaviour can lead to default in SHGs that enjoy external funding, a problem that is sometimes referred to as the 'hot-money cold-money' problem, where the hot money is the members' own highly valued savings and the cold money is the less-valued external fund.

Long-term thinking

Perhaps the most striking difference between SHGs and un-assisted clubs is in their attitude to the life-span of the club. Because unassisted ASCAs are there just to swap a series of small pay-ins for a few big pay-outs, their members are prepared to close them down when anything threatens that goal, perhaps to restart with new membership a little later. As time goes by there are many reasons why closing down becomes a sensible course of action, as we saw in the third chapter. But SHGs (or their promoters) tend to have multiple goals, some of which require the SHG to stay around in the long term – permanently, if possible.[10]

An NGO and its donor make a considerable investment in setting up an SHG, an investment that is not rewarded, as is an ordinary business, with income. The fruits of development-oriented SHG investment are measured in 'impact': the degree to which women have become truly empowered, the degree to which their family incomes have risen and the extent to which their voice has become more influential in the home and in the community, and so on. Measuring all this is not only a very difficult but also a costly and time-consuming task, adding to the need to keep the SHGs running long enough to ensure that these ends are both met and measured.

SHG promoters also felt under steadily increasing pressure to demonstrate that their financial service work for the poor was as 'sustainable' as other modern alternatives, such as the 'providers' that we examine later in the chapter. Indeed, sustainability has become such a watchword of modern microfinance that it may have blinded us to the more modest but still worthwhile virtues of the transitory. The one thing that SHG promoters fretted about more than anything else was that their groups might break up before their developmental goals were achieved. Consultants were paid to try to guess whether or not this would happen, and to think up ways of ensuring that it didn't.[11]

To improve the chances that their SHGs would survive for the long term, some NGOs began to follow the lead pioneered by the credit union movement. They linked SHGs to 'federations', higher-level bodies designed to counter the pressures that lead indigenous clubs to close down after a year or two. We reviewed the main functions of such a body in Chapter Three: they provide SHGs with a secure home for their surplus savings, with oversight so that clear rules are set and disputes resolved, and with advice and training to run the SHGs professionally. Ideally, they also provide legal identity and protection, and insure members' savings. They can act as a spokesperson and advocate of their SHGs, and some have achieved good relationships with government officials and secured access to government programmes for their members. Knowing that they are members of a wider federation than just their own SHG may encourage members to be more respectful of SHG rules. Federations also tend to have the 'institutionalizing' effect that we noted in Kochi's Annual Savings Clubs and Burial funds – standardizing interest rates and other terms, so that they become better understood and more transparent.

Work to establish, improve and fund these federations is still going on, and has not been easy, as even their advocates admit.[12] They cost money to run properly, and this money must either be raised from SHG members through subscriptions or fees for services, or must come from grants from private or public sources.

Watching from the sidelines, my guess was that SHGs might, through this route, evolve into fully fledged credit unions, joining a movement with a long history of experience of permanent owner-managed savings institutions, but breathing life into it with a new and admirable focus on drawing poor and very poor people in as members. To some extent that is happening. The organization Cooperative Development Foundation (CDF, undated), for example, from southern India, promotes 'thrift cooperatives' (a form of credit union) among poor men and women, and helps them learn how to save as fast and as much as possible, and to turn those savings into loans among themselves as safely as possible. They generally do not take outside 'cold' money.

But my guess was mostly wrong. Instead, SHGs have gradually played down self-management and ownership and have preferred to turn themselves into groups of clients of formal lenders. Most SHGs have, rather successfully, become channels for formal bank loans to middle and low-income groups.[13] Indian banks are required by law to direct a proportion of their lending to disadvantaged groups, a category that includes SHGs, so it suits banks to do business with them. It suits the clients, too: under other circumstances getting a bank loan isn't easy, but forming a SHG is not so hard, and once the formalities are gone through a loan is normally forthcoming. Increasingly, banks themselves send their officers out to organize these borrowing groups. Lending to SHGs is not a particularly profitable part of the banks' business, but it is the easiest way to discharge their statutory obligations to the poor, and banks can get the loans refinanced cheaply by NABARD and others. Moreover, banks generally enjoy better on-time repayment rates on their loans to SHGs than in other parts of their lending business, an outcome which is helping to restore India's historically rather poor loan repayment discipline. Nevertheless, if the SHG system is to go on growing, interest rates or other charges paid by SHG members will need to rise in order to keep subsidies small enough for public funds to afford.

Several research reports have shown that as bank borrowing becomes more and more the principal role of SHGs, other functions drop away, and SHGs become conduits rather than institutions.[14] Members tend to save only the minimum needed to lodge with the bank to secure the loan, and most do not regard their SHG itself as a safe and useful place to save (World Bank, undated,b). Consequently, lending to members from their own savings has dropped off:[15] most loans are sourced from the bank. To the distress of some NGO activists, the social developmental work of the SHGs is taking more and more of a back seat.

It is a fascinating history. Over a period of 20 years or so, a simple indigenous saving club was discovered by activists who explored its social and political potential. Later, government, bankers, and SHG members themselves have steadily transformed it into a channel for formal bank lending to hundreds of millions of poor and not-so-poor people. Three trends run through this and through many of the examples we examine in this chapter. First, as systems scale up, social development goals give way to financial intermediation as the main reason for the system's existence, simply because it turns out that that is what the users most value. Second, costs are met less and less out of the public purse and more and more by commercial prices paid by the users. And third, when poor people are offered a genuine choice of financial services, they are able to compare attributes such as relevance, convenience, returns, and risk: they may then prefer to buy services from reliable providers than to go to the bother of setting them up for themselves.

Village banks: independent village-level institutions of the poor

FINCA, the Foundation for International Community Assistance, was formed in Latin America in the 1980s by professionals with an interest in financial services for poor people. In 1989 it published a *Village Banking Manual*, authored by John Hatch, which set out, with great simplicity and clarity, a model savings-and-loans club that could be run by poor women with initial help from outsiders. The club was called a 'village bank'. It had many similarities with unassisted user-owned clubs, and was clearly based on the dynamics of what I have called 'basic personal financial intermediation': it helped poor people systematically turn their savings into usefully large lump sums.

The model proved attractive to many NGOs and their donor supporters,[16] who were seeking a way of fostering community development through popular participation. Through these NGOs, village banking spread, first through Latin America and then further afield, especially in Africa. In the run up to the 1997 'summit' there were more than 5,000 village banks with more than 100,000 members (nearly all women) in more than 30 countries. They had savings balances exceeding four million dollars and loans outstanding of more than twice that figure.

Like many Indian SHGs, village banks blended 'hot' and 'cold' money: members' savings and external finance. But whereas SHGs normally started with savings, village banks began with an injection of cash from the promoting NGO. This cash kicked off a cycle of saving and borrowing that enabled the members to build their own funds, allowing the promoters to take back the 'cold money' and to leave, having set up an independent, self-financed and self-managed permanent village-level institution. The system was attractively neat and logical: it had the internal coherence and cyclical 'completeness' that make the ROSCA so appealing. Here's how it worked, using an example of a village bank with 30 members.

The NGO starts the ball rolling by lending to the 'bank' (the group of women) a sum of money – say $1,500 – that is immediately divided among the members so that each gets a loan of $50. The members repay these loans, with interest, to their bank (that is, to themselves as a group) on a weekly instalment basis over 16 weeks. At the end of the 16 weeks the bank repays the whole amount, along with the interest, to the NGO. Village bankers called this flow of cash, from the NGO through the bank to the members and then back again, the 'external' account. By repaying on time, the bank becomes eligible for a second external loan, on similar terms and again with a 16-week cycle.

The members of the bank simultaneously run an 'internal' account, built from their own money amassed through regular weekly savings: over the 16 weeks each member saves a sum equal to 20 per cent of her loan. In our example, this would be $10 per member, for a total savings for the bank of $300 saved during the first loan cycle. This money stays in the bank, and is available for lending to members, as in an ASCA. Members repay these internal loans with interest, causing their internal fund to grow steadily.

The NGO increases the value of its loans to the bank each cycle (usually by the amount that the members have saved in the previous cycle, to further encourage savings). So, in our example, the second cycle loan made by the NGO would be $1,800 ($300 more than the first cycle loan): each member will get a second loan of $60. The cycle repeats until seven cycles have been completed. By this time the internal fund will have become substantial, fed by savings and by interest on internal account loans. The village bank has become fully independent, and the NGO can end its involvement as a bank financier.

Figure 5.1 shows the regular progress of the seven external loans and their repayments, as well as the individually tailored 'internal' loans taken by the member featured in the chart. (For simplicity the chart is presented in monthly rather than weekly intervals, so we see four monthly instalments, instead of sixteen weekly ones, for each cycle).

A notable feature of village banks, clearly visible in the diagram, is that the values of the loans rise steadily, and so do the repayments and interest made on them. This reveals

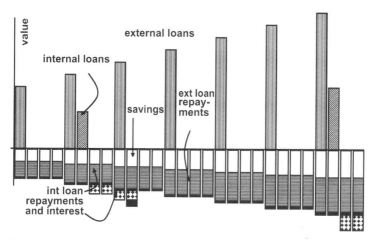

Figure 5.1 Original village bank

an important assumption of the model: that loans will be invested in small businesses that quickly and continuously create the capacity to save larger and larger sums out of business profits. These are assumed to be mainly trading businesses. The model is, therefore, not just a financial services model aiming to help the poor turn a series of small sums into large sums. Rather it is a *small business promotion* model, aimed at helping the poor overcome poverty through assisted investment in business ventures. We saw this in some Indian SHG promoters, and we will see it again when we look at 'providers' later in the chapter.

NGOs that set up village banks are interested in social and economic development goals, above all the participatory ownership and management of institutions by the poor and the development of poor-owned businesses. However, they also need to get back the money they lend to the banks, to fund more village banks elsewhere. For good loan repayment they depend primarily on 'peer pressure'. A loan is not disbursed until the previous one is repaid in full. So the bank, a sort of collective of 30 women, has to be able not only to handle the collection and storage and use of the repayments it receives from members, but to enforce repayment. It can do this by warning bad payers that if they don't repay on time then the next external loan will be delayed, causing inconvenience to all the members. If the shame of this isn't enough to persuade the recalcitrant member to pay up, the group can decide to expel her, or, sometimes, collect the money due by confiscating some of her goods.

This represents an articulated, specific threat based on the common-sense bargain that underlies all unassisted clubs such as ROSCAs or ASCAs. In them, it is obvious to all those who take part that the thing just won't work unless everyone pays in as well as takes out. The risk of nonpayment is well understood and need not be articulated until something threatens to go wrong. But when, as in a village bank, external funds are involved, the bargain is less clear because *three* parties are now involved: the individual member, the club, and the NGO, and the relationship between them is not so obvious and not so familiar. Unsurprisingly, three-way use of peer pressure has often proved problematic. As we shall see later, providers in Asia started using a strong form of peer pressure ('joint liability') enthusiastically, but many have since given it up.

We can't make a direct comparison between the success rates in the use of peer pressure of unassisted and of promoted groups, because the most common way that unassisted clubs tackle problems is to close the club before the problem becomes severe, or to shun leaders or managers or members of clubs that have 'gone bad'. This simple but effective use of a 'survival of the fittest' policy is rarely available to the promoters of SHGs and village banks. They make considerable investments (not least of pride) in their groups, and are reluctant to see them break up.

From promoter to provider

Our description of the village bank was of the original model, from the 1980s. Later, many variations came about, often in response to issues discussed in this chapter. The most conspicuous trend has fundamentally changed the nature of many village banks from user-managed institutions to groups of retail customers.

I saw this for myself during a trip to East Africa in 2000. There, I found NGOs who, though they used village bank technology, had dropped the idea of fostering independent user-owned institutions and wanted to turn themselves into permanent providers of financial services to the poor. I naively asked one NGO branch manager to tell me about the progress of the 'internal account', the fund built from savings and owned by the members themselves, that is supposed to allow bank members to become self-sufficient so that the NGO can move elsewhere. Very politely, the manager told me that while at one time her purpose had been to help members build up this fund and operate autonomously, her ambitions were now quite different. She now wanted to maintain her branch as a permanent supplier of financial services to the members, and as such she saw the loans disbursed from the internal account as competition for the branch's own loan business. She said, 'We would like to take over the loan business done by the internal fund'.

In late 2000 NGOs that used the village bank method got together to update their aims and methods. They published a summary of their deliberations in a 2002 booklet called *New Directions in Poverty Finance: Village banking revisited* (Churchill et al. 2002). It presented village banking as a broad federation of organizations using finance to improve the lives and livelihoods of as many poor people as possible by whatever methods were most likely to prove effective. That meant that the ambition to create independent village-level banks was played down,[17] and the retailing of financial services directly to poor people took over as the fastest-growing activity. Village banking, like the SHG movement, was moving away from 'promotion' towards 'provision'.

Meanwhile, NGOs that had adopted the 'provider' rather than the 'promoter' approach from the very start were making astonishing headway, especially in Asia.

The Providers

A better kind of moneylender

We now come to the world's most famous banker to the poor. Muhammad Yunus and his creation, the Grameen Bank of Bangladesh, jointly won the Nobel Peace Prize for 2006, but even before that their names had gained worldwide recognition. The citation for the Nobel award notes the bank's efforts 'to create social and economic development from below'. In stressing the social side of Grameen's work the citation echoes the impetus behind SHG and village bank promoters, and Yunus has been very clear that, for him too, the aim of microfinance is not profit-maximizing banking but the elimination of poverty and the promotion of a just society (see his recent book, Yunus 2008).

Like SHGs and village banks, Grameen sets up groups, normally of about 40 people, all of them women from households that are known to be poor through checks on their landholdings and income. From its start in 1976, Grameen has been a 'provider' rather than a 'promoter'.[18] It did not ask the poor to manage their own services. Its groups are customer groups, brought together each week to facilitate a retail loans service. Loans go to individuals directly from the bank, and not to the group to divide up among its members. Group members cross-guaranteed each other's loans,[19] but the group does not own the fund out of which the loans are made.

Grameen Bank provides loans (a 'saving-down service' as we would say) to a mass market. From the user's point of view what Grameen Bank does is similar to the urban moneylender we reviewed in Chapter Two. Figure 5.2 illustrates Grameen's methods as they were in the 1990s (there have been changes since which we recount later).

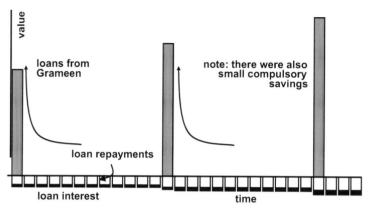

Figure 5.2 Grameen I model

Like the urban moneylender, Grameen offers a lump sum which is recovered in a series of small payments. In Grameen's case in the 1990s this was invariably fifty weekly payments over one year. Like the moneylender, Grameen takes interest, but instead of deducting it at the time the loan is given, Grameen takes it in small easy-to-find instalments along with the weekly repayments. As with the moneylender, most clients immediately embark on a fresh loan cycle as soon as one cycle is complete. Indeed, Grameen usually insists on this.

The similarities with the urban moneylender are striking, but the differences are more important. Grameen selects poor clients out of a social mission rather than as a business strategy. Like the promoters of village banks, Grameen required the clients in the group to cross guarantee each other's loans, whereas moneylenders rarely use guarantees of this sort, preferring to rely for good repayment on their personal knowledge of the client and the client's dependence on them for future loans. Grameen charges a much lower rate of interest on loans than the moneylender. Grameen's 'flat rate' interest system requires a small fixed interest payment each week. They total 10 per cent of the face value of the loan, but since the loan is paid off in weekly instalments the average value of the loan in the client's pocket is half the face value, so the interest rate on an annualized basis (see Chapter Two) is twice the nominal rate, or an APR of about 20 per cent.[20]

The main problem poor people face with moneylenders, however, is not the price of loans but their availability: the poor find it hard to persuade someone to give them an advance. This is where Grameen really scores, because once a client is a member of a group she is guaranteed access to a series of advances, as long as she repays on time and her fellow-members do the same. To secure this unusual right, Grameen clients struggle, sometimes at considerable cost, to maintain their repayments.[21] Moreover, Grameen Bank differs from the moneylender in being a professional organization with a massive outreach. It had around two million clients by the mid 1990s (it reports its progress monthly at Grameen, undated,b).

Grameen Bank's 'members' loved it, and our understanding of the money management needs of the poor tells us why. They had a system under which a year's worth of weekly savings, small enough to be affordable from ordinary weekly cash flow, is swapped for a substantial lump sum that can be used for whatever purpose is a priority at the time – an emergency, a life-cycle event, or an investment. So far so good, but what made Grameen's service so remarkable was that it was local, cheap and above all *reliable*. The youngsters who worked as Grameen field staff came to the village every week, in monsoon rain or in the heat of summer, and they didn't ask for bribes. Unlike SHG or village bank members, Grameen members had no management to do: all the bookkeeping and other paperwork was done, reliably enough,[22] by Grameen, and all the members had to do was to show up each week with their repayments. There was a price to pay for this, of course, but at a fee rate of 10 per cent (10 taka for each 100 taka transacted) or an APR of about 20 per cent (see above), it seemed a miraculously cheap price.[23]

At first, social and financial development work ran alongside each other in Grameen. For example, members were asked to build shelters that would house the weekly meeting of the microcredit group but also serve as elementary schools, and during discussion sessions at meetings members were helped to learn how to manage their school. But as time went on, the schools fell away, and the discussion sessions in the meetings became briefer and now have all but disappeared. Rather like SHGs, Grameen groups have evolved to focus sharply on their financial role.

Loans for businesses?

Like the promoters of village banks, Dr Yunus believed that loans should be invested in starting or expanding businesses, and thus set off an upward spiral of investment and income, allowing the client to service ever-bigger loans (Yunus 1982). Some clients do indeed start or expand businesses, but as we saw in Chapter One poor people's needs for lump sums are so varied and numerous that they are unlikely to use all or even most of their loans for business uses. Research that I have carried out in the villages confirms this (Rutherford 2005b).

It is easy to suppose that members *should* invest in businesses: if not, where does the money come from for the repayments? But as members of ROSCAs know, and as we have learned from observing them in earlier chapters, it doesn't matter what you spend your lump sum on as long as you can make the periodic payments out of your normal cash flow.[24] By asking for loans to be repaid in very small weekly bites, Grameen made it easy for households to find those repayments, or to borrow from neighbours in weeks when they couldn't. Ironically, this brilliant device – small frequent repayments – turned what was advertised as an enterprise-development credit programme into a vastly more popular and usable general loan service that could be enjoyed by millions of poor households who did not invest in businesses.

But there was a catch, one that led to dramatic changes for Grameen. Assuming that its members *were* investing virtually all of their loans in businesses, Grameen, like village bank promoters, raised the value of the loan, and hence the value of the weekly repayment, at each loan cycle. Households had to ensure that their budget also grew each cycle: if not, there is bound to come a time when the value of the weekly repayments exceeds the capacity to pay them. It would have been sensible for members whose budgets *were* expanding – perhaps because they really were investing in businesses – to accept the bigger loans, and for others to keep their loans within their budget limits. But in the environment of the weekly meeting, that proved difficult to ensure. If everyone else was getting a bigger loan each cycle, it was difficult for an individual to resist the offer[25]: a good example of the psychological dilemmas being investigated in a newish branch of economics called 'behavioural finance' (for examples see Thaler 1994).

And so, where Grameen had been active in a village for many years and loan values had risen to $200 or more, many clients experienced repayment problems and dropped out altogether. Other poor people, seeing this, decided not to join. Our understanding of 'basic personal financial intermediation' explains this neatly: lump sums must equal the accumulated savings of a given period, no matter whether they are 'saved up' or 'saved down'. If that relationship is broken, problems arise. In indigenous clubs like ASCAs and ROSCAs, where all the money has to come from their own pockets, the loan inflation problem doesn't arise. But where 'hot money' is on offer, as in Grameen's case, the natural balance that disciplines these clubs is distorted.

Before we look at what Grameen did about the problem, we need to complete our brief discussion of business lending. Of those Grameen members who *do* invest in businesses, many have done very well indeed. Those 'rags to riches thanks to microfinance' stories that you've seen in the newspapers or on television are usually true, even if they don't represent the typical Grameen borrower. My own fieldwork suggests that half or more of the value of all microfinance lending is used in some kind of 'income generating activity', very broadly defined. However, that money is used by a small minority of borrowers. That makes sense: those with successful businesses gear up their loans quickly without running into difficulties.[26] In any village you will find a few traders or small producers who take the lion's share of microfinance lending, and do well with it. It is to the movement's credit that it tries to serve both the poor in general, with general purpose loans, and small business-people with enterprise loans, and recent changes made by Grameen, described below, has allowed them to get better at doing both.

The kind of lending that Grameen does in Bangladesh is sometimes called 'poverty lending', because it selects its group members, and therefore its borrowers (since all group members have the right to borrow) on the basis of their poverty rather than on the basis of their business acumen. Elsewhere, especially in eastern Europe, West Asia, and Latin America, enterprise-microfinance programmes deliberately seek out borrowers with businesses or with business potential. They tend not to be among the poorest. If a microfinance organization's website advertises that it is serving the 'economically active poor' that probably means that it focuses on business lending. These programmes, excellent though many of them are, do not feature in this book, since our focus is on how the mass of ordinary poor people manage their money, and not on entrepreneurs.

Second generation Grameen

By the end of the 1990s many of Grameen's clients found themselves in the loan inflation trap. The bank had lent them too much too quickly and they fell behind in their repayments. Many stopped attending the weekly meeting altogether. All this drove Grameen to change its approach, so that early in the new century Grameen became more than just a friendly moneylender. It added deposit collection services, and in both its lending and its deposit collection it developed a level of flexibility that made its services even more convenient to use than those of its informal rivals. The changes, which the bank launched under the name 'Grameen II' (Yunus 2002), to distinguish it from 'classic Grameen', rescued it from near bankruptcy, greatly expanded its business, and strengthened its balance sheet. By the latest count, in January 2009, it has more than seven and a half million clients, is chalking up regular surpluses, and is financing all of its loans from deposits collected from the public.[27] It has become a 'proper' intermediary bank, but one that continued to serve (mostly) poor people.

Compared to 'classic Grameen', Grameen II makes loans more usable by granting them for a variety of terms rather than the invariable one year, and allowing some flexibility in the previously rigid repayment schedule. It also allows loans to be 'refreshed': so that, when a loan is part-repaid, the borrower can borrow again the amount so far repaid, providing extra liquidity that is very helpful to poor borrowers on small and unreliable incomes. The group guarantee has been abandoned: it had the effect of penalizing good clients for the shortcomings of not-so-good ones, and made no commercial sense. Customers who pay on time can now be sure of getting repeat loans, no matter how others in the group behave. Finally, loan officers have learned not to pressure borrowers to increase their loan value each year, and have become better at estimating their customers' cash flows and making sure that loans and repayment schedules are in line with what the member can pay.

But the biggest changes came with Grameen II's new savings services. Yunus had long believed that savings were of limited value to the poor.[28] With Grameen II he changed his mind, and Grameen became a leader in pro-poor savings. Figure 5.3 illustrates the flows of cash in Grameen II.

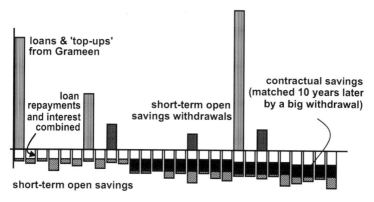

loans & 'top-ups' from Grameen

loan repayments and interest combined

short-term open savings withdrawals

contractual savings (matched 10 years later by a big withdrawal)

short-term open savings

Figure 5.3 Grameen II model

Two parallel savings systems are in play, one short-term and one long-term. The short-term service is an open access savings account, into which members can pay whatever they like each week, and withdraw whatever they like, subject to a few limiting conditions.[29] This makes it rather like a current account at a regular bank, and like those accounts it features very high transaction flows (members put in and take out a lot of money during the year) but rather low balances (over the course of time they take out almost everything they put in).

The second saving service is a 'commitment' account.[30] It features regular equal monthly deposits over a long haul of ten years, after which the saver takes back the deposits plus interest. It pays a 'real' rate of interest (a rate higher than the inflation rate) so members' savings increase their value: after ten years the nominal value almost doubles. The lowest monthly deposit allowed is quite small, so even very poor savers can open an account, and those with slightly more resources can open a bigger one or open several smaller ones with varying maturity dates. There are rather few equivalents of this commitment account in the world of informal finance: the closest is the South Indian marriage fund, described in Chapter Four. This is because informal finance, with its generally sensible preference for time-boundedness, is ill-equipped to handle transactions over the long term. Grameen II's commitment savings, therefore, offers poor savers something they can get nowhere else, and this has greatly contributed to its popularity.[31]

The core service

To understand the full importance of Grameen II we need to think about all three of its basic services together. They offer a complementary set of ways to convert a series of savings into a lump sum, the process that is at the heart of basic personal financial intermediation for poor people. Together, they constitute what I call the 'core service':

First, the open-access savings service allows you to make frequent, multiple, small-scale swaps. As long as you save a little each week, there's usually something in the account that can be withdrawn to take care of a food shortfall, to handle a sudden need to visit the doctor, or to make a Grameen loan repayment in weeks when you're short of cash.[32] The account rivals the 'reciprocal' swapping of savings between neighbours and family that, as we saw in Chapter One, is the single most common financial activity of poor people.

Second, the Grameen II loan provides you with a way to create a more substantial sum either for a planned use such as a life-cycle event or a business investment, or a sudden emergency need, and lets you repay it in bite-sized weekly instalments. It is a more professional version of the urban moneylender we reviewed in Chapter Two.

Third, the commitment savings account gives you the chance to make a really long-term high-value swap, suitable for family ambitions like education, marriages and jobs for the youngsters, land and housing, and more distant anxieties like how to survive after you are too old and weak to work. It is better than Jyothi's savings service (Chapter

Two) and more like a managed club like the South Indian marriage funds (Chapter Four).

All three of these services are offered conveniently, flexibly and reliably; three attributes of money management that all of us demand but which the poor rarely enjoy. Services are delivered right there in the village, at frequent weekly intervals, with enough flexibility to suit the cash flows of most poor households. Professional management ensures reliability: in general the bookkeeping is accurate, the service is delivered on time and without the need to bribe, and promises to disburse loans or return savings are kept. Moreover, Grameen offers 'saving down' (borrowing) opportunities affordably, with a 'price to sums-transacted' fee of around 10 per cent (about 20 per cent APR), and it rewards long-term 'saving-up' with positive real rates of interest.

If we cast our minds back to Chapter One, where we reviewed the money-management dilemmas of poor people and saw how inescapable is their need to turn their savings into lump sums, we can appreciate why it is that Grameen and its competitors in the villages and slums of Bangladesh are so wildly popular.

Microfinance on Wall Street

ASA, the Association for Social Advancement

The 'core service' that we have just described – giving poor people multiple chances to turn savings into lump sums in various ways over varying periods – is at the heart of microfinance success, and few providers have understood that as well as ASA, the Association for Social Advancement, one of Grameen's leading competitors in Bangladesh. A latecomer to microfinance (it had started life trying to incite peasants to take over the government), ASA in the 1990s simplified and standardized Grameen's methods, and made them more cost-effective. Its practical-minded creator, Shafiqual Haque Choudhury, trained his staff to focus on the essentials: getting the lump sums out and the payments in. Their success pushed ASA to the top of the first-ever list of the world's best microfinance providers assembled by Forbes magazine, an American business newspaper (Forbes 2007). The Forbes' list appeared in late 2007, about a year after Yunus and Grameen were awarded their Nobel Prize. The Nobel committee cited Grameen's success in 'social and economic development from below', but Forbes' listing was based unambiguously on commercial banking criteria. ASA was at the head of the list because it earned the best combined scores in measures of scale (the value of its loan portfolio), efficiency (the costs of doing business), risk (the likelihood that their loans would be repaid) and return (profits).[33]

Second to ASA in Forbes' worldwide list was Bandhan, an Indian NGO that adopted ASA's super-efficient delivery systems and had been coached by ASA. It is among India's fastest-growing microfinance institutions (Arora 2009). Providers in India like Bandhan[34] started later than the SHG promoters but they are growing faster and creating more business-like institutions. The promoters of first-generation SHGs, working hard to help illiterate women manage their own finances, cannot compete, in financial services, with Bandhan-like providers who manage a standardized intermediation process and reap the benefits of scale. Scale also helps Bandhan outpace the small local banks who serve second-generation SHGs. The future for microfinance in India almost certainly lies with providers like Bandhan.

The Nobel committee, looking back on Grameen's 30 years of work, saw microfinance through a late-twentieth century lens, focused on human development goals. Forbes saw microfinance as it is now becoming: a business to be measured by business yardsticks. The difference is sharp, and its symbolic importance huge. But it reflects how the international perception of microfinance is changing rather than any real difference in how Grameen and ASA actually practise microfinance. Both organizations do their 'development' work through the provision of financial services rather than through social or political projects, and both aim to maximize scale and efficiency, to control risk, and to make surpluses. Grameen, too, featured in the Forbes 'Top 50' list.[35] To Bangladeshi households their services look similar.

But from the perspective of the international finance industry, general-purpose financial services for poor people is a novelty, one that has drawn them to seek alliances with proven successes like those on the Forbes list. What is happening to ASA is a good example. ASA, still a Bangladesh-registered NGO, has become the co-owner, with a European finance house, of a for-profit company that manages a multi-million dollar fund to carry the ASA core service into other big potential markets where there are millions of poor households with little or no access to money-management services. China, India, Nigeria, Indonesia and Vietnam, for example, are in their sights. Major European and North American pension managers have invested in the fund, and representatives from the world's big banks make their way to ASA's headquarters in a suburb of Dhaka to interest its founder, Shafiqual Haque Choudhury, in gearing up the fund's capital with their loans.

Not all the pioneers are wholly happy with these developments. Grameen has also linked up with international investors, but prefers to take funds, where possible, from 'social entrepreneurs', entities and individuals who favour 'double bottom lines' that rate social progress as important as profit. Otherwise, fears Muhammad Yunus, Grameen's Nobel laureate, the social aims may get forgotten, and microfinance may fall foul of the greed that, as the recent 'credit crunch' has shown, tarnishes international finance. The argument came to public attention in 2007 when Compartamos, a very successful Mexican microfinance provider, put part of itself up for sale on the Mexican stock exchange. Compartamos was founded as an NGO and later transformed itself into a formal bank. It went for growth, and found tens of thousands of poor Mexican households willing to pay APRs of 70 per cent or more for a basic 'saving down' loan service. Its profits ballooned, and when it listed on the market it attracted massive amounts of money, turning its backers, who included some staff of the original NGO, into millionaires overnight. Somewhat embarrassed, given all the talk about poverty, the microfinance industry went in for a bout of introspection.[36]

New possibilities

Exciting and gossipy as it is, the story of 'microfinance on Wall Street' is not what this book is about. But the arrival of international finance may open some new possibilities to poor users, and we should review them from the perspective of the poor's money management needs. Most obviously is the direct effect on increasing the sheer number of poor people likely to be reached: ASA's ambitions worldwide are a good example.

Other new possibilities arise from the various ways in which the new links between microfinance and 'big finance' are being forged, sometimes with the help of modern information technology, as we see in the case of money transfer services. When the microfinance pioneers started their work in the 1970s, the ATM (the automated teller machine) was less than ten years old[37] and was the latest thing in retail banking technology. Most middle-class bank clients still stood in lines in banking halls, or used the mail, to transact. During the last decade or so of the twentieth century, when banking began to adopt new technology at a rapid pace, microfinance mainly stood by. But this century has changed all that. South Asian migrants working in the Gulf, who used to send their remittances home through informal networks can now have them phoned through to the branch of the microfinance provider closest to their village home, faster and cheaper, thanks to partnerships between microfinance providers and international money-transfer businesses. This can help their money-management in very immediate ways, as you will see if you visit a market place in rural Bangladesh. There, you may well find a poor and probably illiterate woman on the phone to her son in Kuwait, sharply reminding him to send the cash that she needs to make her microfinance repayment for that week.

Mobile phones themselves are becoming channels for banking, and developing mass markets among quite poor people. Pioneers can pop up almost anywhere: the Philippines probably won the international race to make mobile banking popular with the poor, with Kenya and South Africa, among others, not far behind.[38] Though phone-banking can as yet manage only certain kinds of transactions, it helps poor people store value and make payments from it quickly and reliably at any time, an important element of 'core' intermediation needs.

Insurance

Of all the new possibilities for the poor that may emerge from links between microfinance and formal finance, insurance stands out as having the greatest potential but needing the most development. We touched briefly on informal finance's insurance dilemma in Chapters Three and Four when we looked at the fire insurance clubs in Dhaka and the burial funds in Kochi. There is no doubt that the poor need what insurance provides – a way of countering risk. The list of personal and impersonal emergencies that require, suddenly, a large lump sum if they are to be dealt with, is a very long one for the poor. Nor is there any doubt that even the poorest would welcome a chance to insure against life-cycle events that are certain but whose date cannot be predicted: there were more very poor people in Kochi using the 'burial fund' than any other informal financial device in the city. But there are three reasons why informal finance found it hard to develop insurance.

First, informal finance is better at short-term swaps than long-term ones, because holding on to insurance contributions over the long haul is not easy in informal environments. Second, 'true' insurance requires pooling, in which some people receive from insurance much more than they put in while others get little or nothing, and informal devices seldom use this principle, perhaps because it goes against everyday notions of fairness.

Third, insurance by nature tends to be segmented according to specific risks. 'General purpose' insurance, which would cover you for just about anything that happened to you, would be nice, but it doesn't exist and it is hard to imagine how it would. The better-off may be willing to buy a long list of policies, to cover life, health, cars, homes, and so on. But poor people on extremely limited budgets will dislike the fact that some of that expenditure is bound to go unrewarded because the insured risk doesn't occur. They will prefer general-purpose tools, of which long-term saving is the ideal example and borrowing the next best. That is one of the reasons why those elements of the 'core service' are so important: the commitment savings and the general purpose loans that Grameen II clients enjoy in Bangladesh, for example.

It also points to a way-in for insurance. Devices that combine safe long-term saving with insurance have been shown to appeal to poor households. An example is the endowment insurance policy known as 'Gono Bima' ('people's insurance') offered by Delta Insurance in Bangladesh from the 1990s.

Gono Bima was one of the first microfinance schemes with insurance, rather than loans, as its basic product. It was inspired by Grameen's work: its founders wanted to bring to life-insurance for the poor what Grameen had brought to loans for the poor. It used the same powerful principles: frequent regular instalments that allowed the poor to buy cover in small instalments that can be found from the ordinary household cash flow, and a highly simplified and standardized product. Clients paid a small instalment each week for ten years. At the term's end they took it all back 'with profits' (that is, with a share of any income the company had made on its business). But if they died during the term then their heirs received a full payout just as if the term had been completed. Figure 5.4 illustrates the principle.

It was initially very popular, and the scheme expanded quickly. But, though it has since been successfully relaunched, these first trials were beset with problems. Gono Bima expanded its field operations faster than it could learn to manage them properly. Its decision to retain the premium instalments at field-office level and lend them back to clients in a loan programme modelled on Grameen's proved disastrous, since they lacked the know-how to copy Grameen lending (McCord and Churchill 2005). Early on, Gono Bima had wanted to team up with a microfinance lender to offer the service, but was unable to attract a suitable partner. The instinct, though, was sound: now, partnerships between formal insurance companies and microfinance providers are being trialled in several countries, and not just for life-insurance. Schemes for health cover, and even crop and livestock insurance, areas in which fraud and uncertain identity have always been major problems,

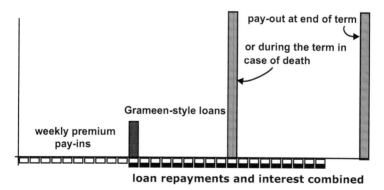

Figure 5.4 Gono Bima loan and insurance model

are being developed. The idea is that the microfinance provider already knows and reaches millions of poor people weekly, while the formal insurance company has the actuarial skills needed to calculate risks and costs, and access to funds. If this combination brings down prices, as it should, poor people will almost certainly buy protection for the most common risks (death, and burial: remember those poor households in Kochi), and may buy others.

Conclusion

In the later twentieth century, concern about world poverty and a growing sense that it must be addressed by working directly with poor people, led many development organizations to explore the use of banking services for the poor as a vehicle for developmental goals.

It isn't easy to measure the impact of programmes of social development, but research reports have credited microfinance programmes with success in alleviating poverty, in improving the position of women, in stimulating small businesses, in increasing the political clout of the poor, and even in boosting health, education, and other critical measures of welfare.[39]

At the same time, and with greater certainty, the programmes have shown that poor people welcome the purely financial services for their own sake. The most enduring success of the microfinance movement has been in finding products and delivery systems that respond to the poor's need for basic personal financial intermediation: to that constant and all-important need to find ways to wring spending power out of small and uncertain incomes.

As a result, microfinance is focusing ever more sharply on its purely financial work. The SHG movement is turning into a way of making sure that India's numerous commercial bank branches do business with the poor. Village banks and their poor clients prosper where good quality loans and savings services are made available on a continuing basis. The Grameen-style providers, for all their early development rhetoric, are popular with their clients because they offer a 'core service' of ways to turn savings into usefully large lump sums of money.

Microfinancial services, well delivered, are so attractive to the poor that they grow rapidly wherever they take root. The established finance industry, which used to be sceptical about microfinance, now recognizes that, and wants a slice of a fast-expanding pie.

CHAPTER 6
Financial lives

Evidence has been collected recently about the complex ways poor people everywhere manage money in their daily lives. 'Financial diaries' point to the universal need for appropriate financial services.

This book has a simple purpose: to describe how poor people manage their money. We began in Chapter One by explaining why it is that people who have so little money need to be so careful about how they manage it. Chapter Two showed how saving – putting money aside whenever possible – is at the heart of money management. The most pressing money management task for the poor is to turn their savings into sums large enough to be useful, whether by saving up, or by taking advances against a promise to repay out of future savings, or by a combination of both. Then Chapters Three and Four reviewed the various tools that they most often use for that job: sharing savings among their neighbours and relatives, running do-it-yourself savings-and-loan clubs, using informal managers, and buying informal money-lending and deposit collection services.

Chapter Five introduced the new organizations that, from the 1970s, began to work on financial services for poor people. The pioneers were motivated by social and economic development goals such as eliminating poverty, improving the resources and status of women, and boosting small businesses. But it soon became clear that what drove the stunning growth of their programmes was the overwhelming response of the poor to the basic money management services: simple loan and savings systems that gave poor people a safe and reliable way to turn their savings into usefully large lump sums.

To tell this story the book has, up to this point, relied on describing the services and devices that the poor use. We have looked at savings clubs, money-lending and deposit-collection, VSLAs and SHGs and village banks and the Grameen Bank, among others, and seen how they relate to the financial needs of the poor. But to show that those needs really *are* important to poor people generally, we need another way to understand their money-management habits, one that looks closely at what real poor people do, day-in and day-out, as they struggle to manage their lives on very small incomes. Finance, as any professor of economics will explain to you, is the intersection of time and money. To get a really sound understanding of financial lives we need to look at both: to follow money through time. We did that in the 'financial diaries'.

Financial diaries

'Financial diaries' is a research method based on a simple idea.[1] Selected poor households[2] are asked to collaborate with field researchers to keep a running record – a sort of diary – of their money. It is done over at least a full year, so as to reveal any seasonal variations, and the researchers visit the households at least once every two weeks and talk to as many people in the household as possible, sometimes privately, sometimes as a family. The aim is to record as many money transactions as possible: of any value, with anyone, and made in any way for any reason. There is a special focus on financial transactions – acts of lending and borrowing, saving and withdrawing, collecting and returning deposits. We also make notes about what the household members say about why they made the transactions, and what they feel about them.

We ran the first diaries in Bangladesh and India between 1999 and 2001, financed by DFID and organized by the University of Manchester (UK). These two efforts were quite small, with fewer than 50 households involved in each country. They were mainly poor households: the incomes of three out of four of them were estimated at less than $2 a day per person, a level that has become a recognized international marker of poverty.[3] Their income came mostly from casual employment and self-employment, including some farming. In 2004-2005 the idea was taken up by a researcher in South Africa who ran a bigger programme there with 150 households, supported by the Ford Foundation, again in collaboration with British aid.[4] More of the South African households had some form of regular income than in Bangladesh and India, either from a wage or from a state grant, and though the households were indisputably poor, a bigger proportion of the households had incomes above the $2 a day level. In all three countries we split our selection of households between urban slums or townships (in Dhaka, Delhi, Cape Town and Johannesburg) and rural areas (in central Bangladesh, in Uttar Pradesh in India, and in the Eastern Cape of South Africa).

Then *MicroSave*, an organization that promotes good microfinance (MicroSave 2009), commissioned a special set of diaries that looked at Bangladeshi households operating accounts with microfinance institutions such as Grameen. These ran for a longer period of three years, from 2002 to 2005, and covered about 50 households. Many of the observations about Grameen and ASA made in the previous chapter come from what we saw and heard while carrying out these 'Grameen diaries' (but see also Rutherford 2009a).

The findings of these four sets of diaries are fully described in reports,[5] and, more recently, in a book, *Portfolios of the Poor* (Collins et al. 2009), so they are not elaborated here. Instead, we shall note a few of the main findings and comment on them in relation to the themes of this book.

The managing poor

Day-in day-out

The diaries confirmed that the poor do indeed manage their money. Not a single one of the 300 or so households lived, literally, 'hand-to-mouth', consuming their income as soon as it came in. In the interval between getting income and spending it, a lot of it was 'managed', meaning that it was pushed or pulled through savings or loans in the form of deposits, withdrawals, loans and repayments. Bangladeshi and Indian households in the sample subjected a sum of money ranging between the equivalent of 75 per cent and 330 per cent of their total annual income to this kind of manipulation. In other words, for every $1 they earned, many households intermediated $2 or more.

Everyone saved in some way, even the very poorest, and they all borrowed. Most saved and borrowed frequently and in a variety of ways. No one used fewer than four different financial tools, and many used a dozen or more. The average household had nine different tools for managing money, and several of the tools were used intensively and continuously.

The most common tools of all were saving at home (in all sorts of places!⁶), and borrowing and lending among neighbours and family. The diary households didn't do this for fun: they needed these tools, as we saw in Chapter One, to ensure that their incomes, always small and often irregular and unreliable, could be stretched to cover the basics of life: food on the table every day rather than just on the days some income came in, and a visit to the doctor when it's needed and not when it's too late. For most poor people, as for the majority of the diary households, the problems of living on just $2 or $3 a day are made much worse by the fact that you don't get that $2 or $3 *every* day: you get more on some days, less on others, and sometimes none at all.

Income irregularity often lay behind the intensity of intermediation in these households. Imagine if they really did earn, say, a reliable $2 each and every day: that would give them a basis to plan on, and, better yet, a basis for potential financial partners to rely on. Shopkeepers would allow them to buy more on credit; and maybe a bank that saw them earning $2 every day would be more willing to chase their savings, or offer them a loan, than if they thought that their income was totally haphazard. But precisely because they don't have income reliability these households are in the greatest need of a place to save and a place to borrow. Many diary households echoed what we said in the first chapter: that those with the least money have, counter-intuitively, the greatest need of financial services. One woman said 'I dislike all this messing with money: running around to borrow, and then having to watch your own savings disappear when someone else comes to borrow them from you. It's unpleasant. But what can I do? When you're poor you just have to do it'. Others mentioned how obsessively important their money-management tasks were for them: 'we lie awake at night worrying about them' said one woman, and her neighbour added 'there's no fear of forgetting any of the amounts we've borrowed or lent: they burn themselves into your mind'.

The bigger challenge

Our diary researchers spent much of their time recording the ins-and-outs of everyday money management. But at the same time the diary households were confronted with the need to create bigger sums, those 'usefully large lump sums' that, as we said in the first chapter, arise unavoidably out of life-cycle needs, emerge suddenly as a result of emergencies, or need to be built in order to take advantage of opportunities and deal with long-term needs.

In Chapters Three and Four we described an array of informal systems used to create larger sums, and the diaries show that they are not just curiosities but are in general use among the poor. As well as providers like moneylenders and deposit takers, we found the full range of savings clubs – saving-up clubs, ASCAs and ROSCAs – in all three countries, actively in use by diary households as we carried out our research. We remarked in an earlier chapter that the distribution of these devices varies by region, and the diaries showed that, too. South Africa had the greatest number of ASCAs: in South Africa they were among the most intensively used of all financial tools, and many households were actively running several of them at one time. Some households in both Bangladesh and India were using ROSCAs, but the auction type of ROSCA we found only in India. On the whole, diary households in the two South Asian countries were more inclined to create large sums through borrowing (or 'saving down'), while in South Africa most were created through saving up, many of them via the savings clubs.

The diaries showed how financial tools were used in combination, something that can't be seen in studies that look just at the tools themselves, or at particular providers, or in the 'one-off' interviews with poor respondents that we find in survey-based reports. To assemble sums big enough to deal with many needs, the households patched money together from as many sources as they had available: from their savings clubs, from loans, and also from selling assets. This 'patching' is another reason for the richness of financial life among the poor, showing us why it is that they tend to have so many deals on the go at any one time.

The diaries also let us appreciate the weaknesses of informal services and devices from the users' point of view. This is seen partly in their doubtful reliability: moneyguards may not return your money when you need it, private moneylenders are notoriously liable to refuse you a loan just when you need it most, and savings held at home can be lost or stolen or frittered away. It is also seen in informal finance's chronic difficulty with building up substantial sums over time: very few of the households had savings clubs or deposit takers that lasted more than a few years at most.

Working with the newcomers

One of the most marked regional differences was, as we expected, in the presence of microfinance organizations. Only in Bangladesh were they common. When the Indian diaries were run, in 2000-2001, MFOs had barely got going there: Bandhan, for example, was founded as late as 2001. Only in one of the Indian village sites where the diaries were run, were a few diary households using an MFO. There were none in the urban sites in Delhi. Nor did SHGs show up significantly in the Indian diaries. In South Arica, MFOs were entirely absent from our data.[7]

In Bangladesh, MFOs were well-entrenched by the time of 1999-2000 diaries. Our researchers found themselves taking notes about as many as 16 of them, and between them these MFOs had reached 30[8] out of the 42 households in the Bangladesh sample. There was clear evidence that MFO accounts were becoming popular. Favourable remarks about MFOs by diary households were most often about the relative reliability of the service (in the sense that MFOs tended on the whole to do what they promised) and the convenience of being able to pay back loans in easy weekly instalments. Unfavourable remarks centred on the rigidities, especially the remorseless insistence on equal exact payments every week without fail, and without prepayments or lump-sum payments being allowed. These kinds of rigidities had forced some diary households, especially the poorest, to close their MFO accounts. It was already apparent that MFO loans were used as general-purpose loans: only some of them went into businesses. And it was clear that the MFOs, collectively, had yet to claim more than a minority share of the financial business of their clients: more of the households' money still flowed through the traditional informal devices and services than through these new semi-formal providers.

A few years later, when we ran the 'Grameen diaries', there was evidence that the situation in Bangladesh was changing. The two sets of diaries can't be directly compared because of differences in the way the households were chosen,[9] but some trends were nevertheless clear. Most obviously, MFO methods had changed. Competition between MFOs had grown and begun to bite. They were no longer able to dictate terms to their customers, but were having to attract them by improving their existing products and introducing a broader range of product types, including more savings. As a result, services had become more user-friendly and more flexible. A few households were beginning to entrust a bigger share of their financial business to MFOs and to reduce their dependence on informal tools, though the number was too small to do more than hint at a trend.

But it was clear from remarks made by the households that the changes the MFO had made were in the right direction, as they saw it. Diary households liked the new open-passbook savings accounts, which made it easier to manage frequent small spending needs. They liked the way MFO loans had become commodities rather than privileges. In the past, an MFO loan was accompanied by a flow of advice from the MFO about how it should be used, but by 2005 MFOs were so eager to satisfy clients that loans were given more speedily, with fewer conditions and little or no lecturing. One poor woman from southern Bangladesh told us that 'these days, it's just like going to the market to buy cabbages: you can buy a loan from whichever MFO you want, and even if you drop out of one they'll still take you back later'.

Of all the novelties introduced by the MFOs the long-term commitment savings accounts, like the one at Grameen described in the previous chapter, may prove, in the long run, to make the biggest difference to the money-management habits of the Bangladeshi poor. This is because it fills one of the most important gaps in informal finance: the desire to build up big sums over the long term when incomes are small. The single most common remark made by the diary households when we asked them about these commitment savings accounts was 'they should have done it years ago'.

Better money management for the poor

In the first edition of this book, published in 2000, much of the final chapter was taken up with suggestions addressed to semi-formal providers and promoters. Happily, developments since then have made much of that redundant. At that time, several arguments that have now been settled were still raging. Some still thought that savings were irrelevant to the poor, for example, while others believed that loans should be used *only* for business, or that the very poor were incapable of using any kind of financial instrument and should be helped through publicly funded welfare programmes. Not everyone was convinced that the poor were able to pay enough for financial services to make them commercially viable, and some still thought that it was immoral to ask the poor to pay at all.

Because we were all still struggling to understand quite how and why microfinance worked, some superstitions persisted. One was that microfinance was only possible with women clients. Another was that joint liability (clients cross-guaranteeing each other's loans) was essential to microfinance, and that it couldn't therefore be successfully offered to individuals. One enthusiast of the Grameen system, holding up his hand with his fingers out-stretched, tried to convince me that since God has given us five fingers, microfinance only works with five-member groups.

Some debates have softened. When Muhammad Yunus at Grameen Bank suggested that credit should be recognized as a human right, others were outraged, reminding him that credit is just another word for 'debt', and redoubling their argument that the poor need savings more than credit. Now, nearly everyone agrees that both savings and loans – and insurance – are important for the poor. In the 1990s there were what seemed fundamental disagreements about the *purpose* of financial services for the poor. For example, arguments about the merits of 'credit-plus' – the idea that credit for the poor is best when offered in conjunction with other services such as business training, health, financial literacy and other forms of education – were quite sharp then but are less so now. That is because although there is plenty of evidence, some of it presented in this book, that microfinance on its own is useful for poor people, it is also true that some projects have had success in combining microfinance with other services.[10]

My own convictions were still vulnerable to doubts. I had made a hobby of collecting examples of the money-management tools of the poor since first discovering savings clubs in the slums of Managua, Nicaragua in the wake of the 1972 earthquake. But despite later work in dozens of countries I still wasn't certain that they were a truly widespread phenomenon until the results from the financial diary projects came in. Then it became clear that money-management truly is a routine and inescapable part of life for most poor people, a finding that should make the provision of good quality financial services as important a priority to policy-makers as good quality services in health or education or law-and-order.

Still, new debates and worries continue to emerge (Dichter and Harper 2007). In countries such as India and especially Bangladesh, where MFO branches are within reach of most rural and urban neighbourhoods, many households join several MFOs at the same time. This has raised fears of over-indebtedness. As MFOs look more carefully at what is going on, they discover that their clients sometimes use their loans to repay other providers. The weaker MFOs may be right to be worried about this, since increasing competitive pressure will surely cause some of them to fail. But alarmist concern about looming over-indebtedness of their clients is almost certainly exaggerated. As this book has shown, the poor have always had to manage money by 'saving down', so we shouldn't be surprised when it is used to service other debt, whether from expensive moneylenders or more affordable MFOs. MFO loans, where repayment is broken down into small bites, is easier to manage than many other forms of debt. The most recent financial diaries in Bangladesh suggest that debt levels in poor households remain modest. Managing money on small incomes tends to be characterized by transaction values that are large compared to balances: money moves in-and-out of the household rapidly rather than accumulating in large financial assets and liabilities. If anything, MFOs need to work harder to build up the balance sheets of their clients: much bigger savings balances wherever possible, but in many cases larger-scale debt, too.[11]

As the authors of *Portfolios of the Poor* argue, earning only a small income is a big enough handicap in itself. There is no need to make it worse by withholding services that make it easier to manage that money well, especially now that the microfinance pioneers have shown that providing those services at an affordable price is possible. Without reliable financial services at hand, poor people faced with an urgent spending need have to sell assets or, worse still, go without. The result is that small symptoms go untreated, turning minor ailments into full-blown health emergencies, and opportunities to invest in goods or marriage alliances or businesses are missed, keeping people poor longer than necessary. The chance to put some savings away in a safe place, or to trade future savings for a loan, can sometimes transform the situation, allowing poor households to bring past and future income to bear on their spending needs, and not just whatever cash they have at hand at the time.

The small number of principles that we believe are essential to good financial services, set out in 2000 in the first edition of this book, still apply, despite the huge and welcome broadening of microfinance since then and the entry of wholly new players, especially from the established finance industry. We end, then, with a recapitulation of them.

Financial services for the poor help them swap their savings for usefully large lump sums of cash through a process of 'saving up', 'saving down', or 'saving through'. *Good* financial services for the poor are those that perform this swap well. This requires:

Products that suit the poor's capacity to save and their need for lump sums:

- so that they can save (or repay) in small sums, of varied value, as frequently as possible;
- so that they can access the lump sums (through withdrawals or through loans or insurance payments) when they need them: short term for some consumption and emergency needs, medium term for investment opportunities and some recurrent life-cycle needs, longer term for other life-cycle and insurance needs like marriage, health-care, education and old age.

Reliable product delivery systems that are convenient for the poor:

- that are reliable, safe, local, frequent and quick;
- that are not burdened with paperwork and other transaction costs; and
- that are transparent in a way that is easy for illiterate people to grasp.

Institutions adapted to delivering good products:

- that are committed to serving the poor (though not necessarily exclusively); and
- that are cost-effective

A healthy environment for financial services for the poor:

- stable macro-economic and financial management by government;
- the rule of law; and
- enabling rather than restrictive legislation governing promoters and providers of financial services for the poor.

Notes

Chapter 1

1. See the World Bank's 'overview' of understanding poverty (World Bank, undated, a) where poverty is related to hunger, shelter, health, education, water supply, and employment, among other things. The Bank also has a 'poverty analysis' site which can be accessed from the page quoted. The persistence of poverty is the subject of reports produced by the Chronic Poverty Research Centre (2009) at the University of Manchester, UK. An older but still useful introduction to the debate about the definition of poverty, available online, is by Simon Maxwell (1999). Robert Chambers (1995) favours a view of poverty that takes the views of poor people themselves into account. Martin Greeley, also of IDS, favours the use of a 'poverty line' based on food consumption. He argues this in relation to financial services for the poor (Greeley 1997).

2. In some languages there are words for the small hidden sum of cash that a woman will try to keep secret. In the slums of Dhaka women use the Bengali word *'jula'*.

3. This book is about the poor in developing countries, but many of the arguments apply to the poor in wealthy countries too. In the United States, Mark Schreiner and Michael Sherraden argue that because the poor miss out on many publicly funded programmes, public resources should be used to help them to save (Schreiner and Sherraden 2007).

4. Understanding that people can save money when it is 'on the way out' (when spending) as well as when it is 'on the way in' (when receiving income) helps to correct a common misperception about the differences between town and country. It is sometimes thought that in the urban slums people can save because they have a variety of sources continually producing income, but rural farmers may get income only at the end of each growing season, and that is the only time they can save. This ignores the fact that in many countries the rural poor are often not farmers, having lost their land. They are day labourers and may earn on a daily or weekly basis. But even those

poor who are farmers go to market frequently – once or twice a month, or even weekly – to buy perishable or expendable items like salt, fresh food, kerosene oil, matches, and so on. The money they use for this can come from several sources, including the sale of short-term farm produce like eggs, chickens, or vegetables, or from income from supplementary work like cutting firewood, or from selling bigger items in which they have stored (or saved) value, such as stocks of grain, pigs or goats. Each such market visit presents an opportunity to save some money, even if this saving simply converts a non-money form of saving (such as livestock) into cash savings.

5. Evidence for the widespread use of 'reciprocal lending and borrowing' comes from the 'financial diaries' that have been carried out in a number of countries including Bangladesh, India and South Africa. 'Financial diaries' are a research technique in which the money management behaviour of households is tracked over at least a year at frequent intervals (usually twice-monthly). These studies find that reciprocal lending and borrowing is the most often-used money-management device, used by virtually all households (Collins et al. 2009, especially chapter 2).

6. For example, when Grameen Bank of Bangladesh introduced a 'commitment savings plan' in which savers were offered a good rate of interest for regular monthly saving, Grameen's famous founder, Nobel prize winner Muhammad Yunus, was surprised at the rate at which poor households saved. Savings held by Grameen rose sharply, and now exceed Grameen's loan portfolio. For the story of Grameen II see Rutherford 2005a.

7. An early essay stressing the importance of savings in financial services for the poor is by Robert Vogel (1984). Dale Adams, an important early critic of subsidized credit schemes, was an editor of the book in which Vogel's essay appeared.

8. For detailed case studies of how the South African poor cope with the cost of funerals, see Collins et al. 2009, especially chapter 3.

9. Buying in quantity can result in savings of 10 to 50 per cent over short term, justifying the use of loans to finance the purchase. C K Prahalad called this extra price for the poor a 'poverty penalty' (Prahalad 2006).

10. Many such banks started as development projects and we will review the work of some of them in Chapter Five. Public interest in them has been fostered recently by the award of

the 2006 Nobel Peace Prize to Muhammad Yunus and the bank he founded in Bangladesh, Grameen Bank. A year later Forbes, an American business magazine, published its first ever ranking of the world's best microfinance providers. At the top of the list came the Bangladesh NGO ASA (Association for Social Advancement), which specializes in financial services for more than six million poor households. An up-to-date study of ASA's emergence and growth can be found in Rutherford 2009a. The Forbes ranking, however, has been criticised for its methodology.

11. As well as selling assets like crops in advance, you can also sell your labour (or that of your children or spouse) in advance. This is common in countries in South Asia, and is found elsewhere. We could list other examples of ingenious ways to get hold of money, but this book sticks to those that are common everywhere, and which involve mainly financial transactions, rather than sales of goods or labour.

12. In some countries pawnshops have been outlawed, sometimes so successfully that some readers from those countries require an explanation of pawning (after which they normally recognize the phenomenon which tends to exist in their 'grey' economies under a local name). A pawn is a movable asset (most commonly a precious metal, above all gold) that is taken as security for a loan by a lender – the 'pawnbroker'. You take your gold ring along to him and he weighs it and gives you, if you're lucky, about 60 per cent of its market value. When you pay him back (with interest) you get the ring back. If you never pay him back he keeps the ring and in the end sells it. Pawning is to the town what mortgaging land is to the countryside – an example of a class of financial services for the poor by which assets can be turned into cash and back again.

13. I first elaborated the idea of 'basic personal financial intermediation' in an essay I wrote with Sukhwinder Arora (Arora and Rutherford 1997) for the Delhi office of DFID (official British aid), but it is no longer available in print nor online.

14. The Economist newspaper (Economist 1994, page 94) defines a financial intermediary as 'any individual or institution that mediates between savers (that is sources of funds) and borrowers (that is users of funds)'.

15. My definition of financial services with the poor first appeared in an essay I wrote for ActionAid and Oxfam (Rutherford 1996). The essay is a collection of (literally) 57 varieties

of financial services for the poor, each briefly described and commented on. Another good discussion of the various types of financial services for the poor can be found in Adams and Fitchett 1992, a collection of papers that includes a piece by a pioneer of research into how poor people handle their money, the admirable but now deceased Fritz Bouman.

Chapter 2

1. The two examples from India in this chapter were investigated in the company of Sukhwinder Arora during fieldwork we carried out for DFID (British official aid) in India. I researched the ROSCA from the Nairobi slums while in Kenya reviewing a microfinance NGO, again for DFID. The example of 'Rabeya's fund' from Bangladesh was first identified by my Bangladesh research assistant S. K. Sinha and then investigated by us jointly. *Safe*Save is an experimental MFO (microfinance organization) that I founded in Dhaka, Bangladesh in 1996 expressly to test the ideas set out in this book. Its fortunes can be tracked on its website (*Safe*Save 2009).

2. Interest is the price paid for the use of a given amount of *money* for a given amount of *time*. Conventionally, to make comparisons easy, the interest rate is 'annualized' – adjusted to state the rate as if the amount of time were a year. But annualizing rates may not be very meaningful when we are dealing with short periods of time. For example, some poor people borrow sums of, say, $10 for a day from market-based traders, so that they can have something to sell sitting on a mat in the market place. At the end of the day they give back $11. They therefore pay a fee of 10%. Though this rate is high, it is affordable, and the poor borrower can usually scrape a living by selling the goods for a few extra dollars. However, if we calculate it as an annualized interest rate it works out at several thousand per cent. This sounds, and is, absurd, since it is based on the very unlikely possibility that the borrower would agree to take out a loan of $10 and hold it for a year at 10 per cent a day.

3. Conventions for expressing interest rates vary and are subject to local regulation. In the UK and USA, for example, the APR (Annual Percentage Rate) is generally used to express the cost of loans on an annualized basis (and takes into account set-up and similar fees as well as interest). A slightly different convention, the AER (Annual Equivalent Rate) is used for sav-

ings, mainly because with savings we are not always dealing with a fixed contract and clients may vary the amount and timing of their deposits and withdrawals.

4. These days, interest rates can be calculated using the routines in spreadsheet software such as Microsoft's 'Excel'. However, there has been confusion about interest rates among some microfinance practitioners and critics, partly because some lenders use 'flat' rates of interest for their loans (as explained in Chapter Five). For that reason this book includes simplified rules-of-thumb for calculating approximate interest rates, as in this example of Jyothi's rates. We mentioned that clients of Jyothi often take longer than the 220 days to repay, in which case the price they pay expressed as a fee remains the same (9 per cent) but expressed as an APR declines the longer they delay.

5 Robert Christen, now heading microfinance for the Bill and Melinda Gates Foundation, discussed what microcredit programmes can learn from moneylenders in Christen 1989. Meenal Patole and Orlanda Ruthven look at urban moneylending from the moneylenders' point of view in Patole and Ruthven 2002. More recently, Howard Jones, of the University of Reading (UK) has described moneylenders' methods in India (Jones 2008).

6. We could calculate the rate using the IRR, or Internal Rate of Return routine. We would enter successive cells in a spreadsheet with the weekly values +850, -100, -100, -100, -100, -100, -100, -100, -100, -100, -100 and then apply the IRR formula and find a result of 3% per period – in this case per week. To annualize 3% a week in the way that banks would in order to satisfy UK regulations would require converting it using the formula *(1 plus the interest rate for the period quoted) to the power of the number of such periods in a year, minus 1*. Under this formula 3% a week is an APR of 365% $((1 + 0.03)^{52} -1)$, making Ramalu's loan look even more expensive. The formula allows for the compounding effect of the weekly payments, an extra cost that can be significant in long-term loans on which interest is paid at short intervals, such as 25 year home mortgages. Since Ramalu's loan term is brief, my 'rule of thumb', which ignores this sophistication, is not inappropriate. Note also that in calculating the IRR it doesn't matter whether we regard Ramalu's loan as one of Rs1,000 on which Rs150 interest was paid 'up front', or (given that Ramalu only got Rs850 in his hand) a loan of Rs850 on which Rs150 interest was paid at sometime

in the ten week term: the arithmetic is the same (+850 is the same as +1,000-150). I am grateful to Ian McKendry and John Burton of DFID for a lively discussion of how best to calculate Ramalu's interest rates (in personal correspondence, facilitated by Sukhwinder Arora in 2000). For a good general discussion on interest rates, see Rosenberg, 2000.

7. ROSCAs are considered in more detail in the following chapter, but a good general book on them is Ardener and Burman, 1995, which focuses on ROSCAs and women.

8. In Bangladesh, as in some other Muslim countries where both Islamic and conventional banking practices are found, interest is sometimes called 'profit'.

9. 5% a month is only roughly equivalent to 60% a year. Using a strict APR calculation, as described in note 7 above, it is 79.5% a year $((1 + 0.05)^{12} -1)$.

10. If you are saving 10 taka a week then over the year you have an average of 260 taka on deposit. On this you earn 60 rupees. 60 is 23% of 260.

11. The need for women to save up for their widowhood is one of many topics well-treated by Helen Todd, writing about Grameen Bank in Todd 1996.

12. For more on *Safe*Save see its website (*Safe*Save 2009), and for more on my own work as a microfinance practitioner (at *Safe*Save and at a rural experiment) see my own website (Rutherford 2009b). The most recent product under trial is called Product 9 (or 'P9') and is described in the Products page of Rutherford 2009b.

Chapter 3

1. I use 'sharing' here rather than 'pooling', preferring to reserve the term 'pooling' for devices like insurance (discussed later in the chapter) where members may get back more or less than they put in.

2. I used 'funds' to describe Rabeya's savings club in Chapter One because that's what their users call them.

3. They may also store the money with a trusted 'moneyguard': someone in their community whom they trust not to cheat them.

4. Such clubs can also be strengthened in a number of other ways, such as issuing regular periodic statements of accounts to members, ensuring that there are at least two different and unrelated signatories to club bank accounts, and so on.

5. These ancient Japanese ROSCAs were in grain rather than cash. Grain ROSCAs have survived into modern times. A fascinating detailed study over many years of ROSCAs (using bidding) in Taiwan is in Vander Meer et al. 2009.
6. In addition to Ardener's article, see Fritz Bouman's work (Bouman 1979 and 1995).
7. When I was working as a trainee architect in an engineering company, each month on pay-day, all the young men in the office put a set amount of their salary into a special bank account set up for the ROSCA. Whenever the balance in the account grew large enough to buy a Brazilian-made Volkswagen Beetle, we bought one and decided by lottery which of us should have it.
8. Such patterns of reciprocal obligation characterize many other cash exchanges that are not strictly speaking 'clubs'. There are arrangements such as the *neota* (a Hindi word meaning 'invitation') of northern India, in which families are duty-bound to contribute cash for weddings among their neighbours, and then expect to receive the same help when they have a wedding. It is summarized in Rutherford 1996.
9. In some auction ROSCAs only the 11 non-winners would share this discount.
10. Well, actually, not quite, since he put in more in the last four months than he did in the first four. This will skew things slightly in his favour compared to my calculation above. The inverse is true for the first member.
11. During the course of research for the development NGO ActionAid, in 1997.
12. Of course, members who bid high also, like the net savers, enjoy high returns on their deposits, thus offsetting their costs somewhat.
13. Nevertheless, as Sukhwinder Arora points out, care must be taken with using auction ROSCA bids as an indicator of the local price of money, since the bid is also influenced by factors internal to the ROSCA, such as its time period.
14. Sukhwinder Arora's father, who lives in Delhi, confirms that this was true in 1962 when he joined his first auction ROSCA there.
15. I borrow this turn of phrase from John F.C. Turner (Turner 1972) an anarchist writer on housing.
16. Not practised by *all* rickshaw ROSCAs.
17. Genetic science is beginning to favour the latter explanation, whereas traditional archaeology has long accepted the

former. Perhaps we should think of ROSCA types as 'memes' – the intellectual equivalent of the gene suggested by Richard Dawkins (Dawkins 1976).

18. In Bangladesh, for example, two major industries have started up and grown rapidly in the last 30 years: ready-made garments and microfinance. ROSCAs have colonized the factories of the first and many of the offices of the second, where staff find them useful.

19. Disciplined individuals can make use of the lump sums formed in a series of short-term devices like ROSCAs and ASCAs and build them successively into a very large sum for retirement or other long-term need. But they are still faced with the problem of deciding where best to store that cash and how to resist the temptation of drawing down on it. That is another reason why much long-term saving is still done in kind (gold, land, building, and so on) rather than in financial assets.

20. In 'large part' because the club may choose to recover running costs from some of the loan interest income.

21. Moderate, that is, in relation to runaway inflation seen in some Latin American countries. In India, annual inflation rates have been above 10 per cent in some years.

22. Assumes interest is paid monthly at the meetings and is immediately lent out. These figures are all somewhat simplified, and are therefore approximations. Readers with a lot of patience and a good spreadsheet can recalculate the exact figures.

23. $23,177,017. Each of the 24 members will have become almost a millionaire.

24. Some clubs also have entry fees, fines for late attendance, etc.

25. Many co-operatives in The Philippines *do* run well, of course. Indeed, the country has been an innovator in credit co-operatives.

26. As it happens, northern Filipinos found another way of addressing the problem. This is the *ubbu-tungngul* – a device so intriguing that it gets its own description in the last section of this chapter.

27. In the 1980s and 1990s, soon after 'microcredit' got going in a substantial way in Bangladesh, Bolivia and elsewhere, there was a great deal of speculation about whether these services could be run profitably. Several analysts devised methods for working out their 'true' profitability, given that many used

very cheap public funds. A good example is by Jacob Yaron (1994), who proposed a 'sustainability index'. Since then sustainability has remained a badge of success worn by microfinance organizations. Others have argued that there is a legitimate place for subsidy through public funds. For an excellent discussion of this issue in a broad context see Chapter 9 (Subsidy and Sustainability) of Armendariz de Aghion and Morduch 2005.

28. See for example, WOCCU, the World Council of Credit Unions, mainly working with English-speaking groups (WOCCU 2008), and Developpement International Desjardins, mainly with francophone groups (Developpement International Desjardin 2008). There is a large literature on credit unions. Their history (beginning in nineteenth century Europe) is summed up for microfinance fans in Hollis and Sweetman 1998. Montgomery et al. 1996 is a case study of the revitalization of a rural credit union system in Sri Lanka. There are many references to all aspects of credit unions in the Wikipedia entry for them (Wikipedia 2008).

29. I have not seen other discussions of *ubbu-tungnguls* and would like to hear from anyone who has. I discuss *ubbu-tungnguls* and initial investment ASCAs in an unpublished report (Rutherford, no date).

30. Daryl Collins carried out 'financial diary' research in South Africa in 2005 during which this *stokvel* came to light. See Collins 2008.

Chapter 4

1. Sukhwinder Arora and I describe marriage funds and burial funds in Arora and Rutherford 1996.

2. I have been saving weekly, so my average deposit over the three years is $50 (half the total I put in). On that $50 I'm paid interest of $100, or 200 per cent. 200 per cent over three years is equivalent to 66.6 per cent over one year. This is another example of the approximate, but easy, 'rule of thumb' used in this book to estimate the annual rate.

3. The parents of babies who die within three months of birth don't benefit, and the pay-out for minors over three months is half that of adults. Paying Rs15 per thousand per year for life assurance (this was our calculation of the effective cost of such schemes for a six-person household) was expensive relative to the big government-run insurance companies

(life assurance was a public monopoly in India when we studied the burial funds). But the government companies do not turn up at the bereaved household on the very day of the death bearing the cash, a bunch of flowers, and neighbourhood sympathy. Nor will insurance companies return premiums to their customers if the claims they have to meet are less than forecast. Since 2000-01 private life insurance companies have operated in India and have considerably expanded the industry.

4. That is, not just in Hindu societies.

5. In Ghana, for example, there have been attempts to link '*susu*' collectors with banks, and banks themselves have adopted susu-like products (World Bank 1999; CGAP 2008; Allianz Bank 2008).

6. Imran Matin has pointed out to me, on the basis of his work in rural Bangladesh, that many informal rural lenders don't like to take their loans back in small instalments, because they think they'll be tempted to waste them on trivial expenditure. Like their clients, they too prefer 'usefully large lump sums'. Such moneylenders may indeed be lending money out to their safer borrowers as a profitable way of storing savings.

7. I visited them for ActionAid between 1992 and 1997.

8. These examples come from India.

9. Some governments have un-banned it. The Sri Lankan Government, noting the success of private pawnbroking, has gone into the business on its own account, and set up shops around the country. It is said that this has increased competition and brought down the cost of the service. Pawnbroking is well treated in an essay by Fritz Bouman and R. Bastiaanssen (1992). Sukhwinder Arora reports a recent visit to a rapidly growing microfinance organization in Tamil Nadu, India, which is considering acquiring the skills and equipment to begin to give advances against gold to its poor customers.

10. The weight of the *mon* (in India *man* or *maund*) varies from place to place: the standard Indian *maund* is 37.5kg.

11. The *dadon* (tied credit) system for financing fresh-water prawn cultivation in Bangladesh is described in a report I wrote for the NGO CARE (Rutherford 1994): it is unpublished but references to it appear in Ito 2002.

Chapter 5

1. A group of scholars at Ohio State University known as the 'Ohio School', of whom Dale Adams is seen as a leader, became famous for explaining why state-run subsidized rural credit programmes ran into difficulties. See for example Von Pischke 1991.
2. The campaign that the meeting started is still running (Microcredit Summit Campaign, undated).
3. Among the big banks that have been especially active are Citi, Standard Chartered, and Deutsche Bank. For an overview of banks and microfinance, see Harper and Arora 2005.
4. For example, members always sit in the same places at the meetings, to make things easier to remember, and each member has to recall the two or three key points about her own savings and loans, and those of another member. The cash may be stored in a box with multiple padlocks held by different members.
5. This count was made by VSLA Associates, a company formed exclusively to promote the VSLA idea.
6. Private communication with Hugh Allen of VSL Associates, July 2008.
7. These figures are from NABARD (undated). Note, however, that since many people belong to more than one SHG, 'members' is not the same as 'people'. It is not known how many of the SHG savings accounts are dormant: there may be many. APMAS, a national level technical support organization for SHGs, also quotes numbers (APMAS undated).
8. I visited them several times, usually accompanied by Sukhwinder Arora, as part of a series of research trips undertaken for DFID (British Aid) in New Delhi.
9. Others have recently noted the same thing. For example, in a web-based discussion of savings organized by *MicroSave* in July 2008, B. Anjaneyulu's posting read, in part: 'In majority of the SHGs one can see not much difference in the size of the savings in spite of considerable growth in size of the loans over a period of time. The common answer for this from the groups and staff of the promoting institutions is member's wages are very low and hence they cannot save more money. But during our focus group discussions many of these members save at different sources in addition to the SHGs (e.g. local chits (RoSCAs, financial agencies))'.
10. For this reason SHG promoters were not attracted to the ROSCA, the more elegant kind of savings club, which are

inherently time-bound whereas ASCAs can, under some circumstances, last for a long time. See Chapter Three.

11. I know. I've done it.

12. C S Reddy, CEO of APMAS (Reddy 2008) has stressed in a recent interview that supporting federations should be seen as a worthwhile public investment. Sinha 2009 also finds that federations are not yet sustainable.

13. The study by Sinha (2006) estimates that 50 per cent of all SHG members are poor (below the national poverty line). Many middle-income people join SHGs to avail bank loans.

14. Sometimes the conduit is for non-financial benefits as when governments offer people gas connections (for example) as a reward for forming an SHG.

15. There is no central data base of SHG internal saving and lending, so no-one really knows: it is the consensus of most studies that savings and internal lending is dropping off as bank borrowing increases.

16. Support came especially from USAID, the official American aid programme.

17. Nevertheless, the original ideas are still alive and well. In a 2004 lecture John Hatch, who wrote the original *Village Bank Manual*, describes village banks as 'highly democratic, self-managed, grassroots organizations. They elect their own leaders, select their own members, create their own bylaws, do their own bookkeeping, manage all funds, disburse and deposit all funds, resolve loan delinquency problems, and levy their own fines on members who come late, miss meetings, or fall behind in their payments' (Hatch 2004, page 2).

18. Grameen Bank is structured as a bank owned by share-holders. Every customer (group member) buys a share in the Bank and their representatives hold an overwhelming majority of seats on its Board. However, in practice at the village level, most members are unaware of the implications of this and at HQ level control is exercised *de facto* by the bank's professional management.

19. The bank no long enforces 'joint liability' (or 'social collateral') as this cross-guarantee system is known. Indeed, it says it never did so, at least in any 'hard' sense, but that is disputed by some. See Grameen's recent statement on this matter on their website (Grameen Bank undated) .

20 Or somewhat more if we take into account the group tax deductions and the compulsory weekly savings.

21. Because of this, much 'anti-Grameen' literature, in newspapers for example, focuses on cases where women go without food or some other essential in order to repay loans. For a very critical view from a position on the political left see Chowdhury 2007.
22. In fieldwork I discovered some weaknesses in record-keeping, but by-and-large standards are adequate.
23. My understanding of the views of Grameen members comes from long acquaintanceship with many of them, especially as a result of the 'financial diaries' work described in Chapter Six.
24. A chairperson of an ASCA whom Sukhwinder and I met in Cuttack, India, told us that he advises members to invest in anything except businesses, which, he said, are risky and likely to fail, causing repayment problems. He prefers members to buy goods like radios and TVs that can be pawned if repayment problems occur.
25. This was especially the case in the early days when joint liability was (effectively) in use: members argued 'if I am to guarantee the big loans of others, then it's only fair they guarantee my big loan'.
26. Sometimes they borrow the MFO loans of other less entrepreneurial members.
27. And still had a surplus of deposits. In June 2008 total deposits were 138 per cent of total loans outstanding. There are risks here. Grameen has to pay interest on those deposits so it must invest them somewhere. There are already signs that it may be moving too quickly into bigger 'business' loans for its members, some of which may prove unsound.
28. For example, in an address at which I was present in Kuala Lumpur at 'BankPoor 1996', a precursor to the 1997 Microcredit Summit.
29. They *must* pay in a low-value minimum each week. Withdrawals may be restricted if the member is in arrears on her loan. When members take loans, a fraction of the loan is paid into a third savings account that cannot be freely accessed. For details see Rutherford 2005a.
30. Known as the GPS, for Grameen Pension Savings, but by no means always used to build up a pension (and Grameen has no facility to help members buy an annuity when the GPS matures). It is based on the DPS (Deposit Pension Savings) which commercial banks had long offered to their better-off customers and which was wildly popular among them.

31. Handling a mass of low-value savings is not easy. If it is not well done, poor savers can suffer losses. These difficulties, however, are beyond the scope of this book, which focuses on how poor people use the services rather than on the technical complexities of providing them.
32. Savings withdrawals can improve loan repayment rates, something that took Grameen workers time to learn.
33. The list was prepared by Forbes from data collected from MFOs by the Microfinance Information Exchange (www.themix.org), a highly respected data information bank for microfinance. But Forbes' list has been criticised by some because the MIX data is self-reported by the MFOs and may contain errors.
34. Other major provider MFOs in India are Share (www.sharemicrofin.com) and SKS (www.sksindia.com).
35. At 17th overall but 8th for scale of operations.
36. BusinessWeek magazine quotes Yunus on Compartamos: 'They're absolutely on the wrong track,' says Yunus. 'Their priorities are screwed up.' (BusinessWeek 2008). But see also a calm and thoughtful essay by Rich Rosenberg of CGAP (Rosenberg 2007).
37. The first was set up in London branch of Barclay's Bank in 1967, but they did not become widespread until the 1980s.
38. In the Philippines: Rural Bankers Association of the Philippines Microenterprise Access to Banking Services (RBAP-MABS); in Kenya: M-PESA; in South Africa: WIZZIT, all searchable online.
39. Impact is a complex subject. For a two-page briefing see Sharma 2000. For a treatment that puts the issue in full context go to Armendariz de Aghion and Morduch 2005, especially chapter 8. See also Morduch and others' work at the Financial Access Initiative (FAI 2009).

Chapter 6

1. The idea was David Hulme's, and it arose from discussions between him, Imran Matin (of BRAC, a big Bangladesh NGO and MFO) and Stuart Rutherford. Hulme was Director of the Institute for Development Policy and Management at the University of Manchester, UK. IDPM led a consortium of UK universities that in 1999 had won a DFID (British aid) contract to explore the connections between finance and development. The first financial diaries, in Bangladesh and India

were run under this contract. In Bangladesh they were managed by Stuart Rutherford, and in India by Orlanda Ruthven.

2. Where possible the households are selected through participatory wealth-ranking, a technique in which the residents of poor neighbourhoods make their own ranking of who's poorest and who's least poor. Where that can't be done (for example in some Dhaka slums where residents don't know each other well enough) they are chosen at random.

3. They have become well-known as a result of their use in the United Nation's 'Millennium Development Goals' (MDGs), a set of development targets that member nations set themselves in 2000. The $2 a day is per capita, and is measured using Purchasing Power Parity (PPP) rates of conversion between US dollars and local currencies. The broad idea of PPP rates is to compensate for differences in the costs of living in different countries by adjusting rates so that a dollar buys the same amount in each country. When we say that three-quarters of the India and Bangladesh households lived on $2 a day per person or less, we are using these PPP-adjusted rates.

4. Daryl Collins ran the South African diaries. She was supported by Ford Foundation and the FinMark Trust, an initiative of DFID, and by South Africa's Micro Finance Regulatory Council.

5. For Bangladesh, Rutherford 2003; for India Patole and Ruthven 2002, and Ruthven and Kumar 2002; for South Africa Collins 2008 and Collins undated.

6. Commonly in 'piggy banks' of one sort or another (often clay, hence their popular name in Bangladesh, 'clay banks') but also thrust between roofing sheets, pressed into hollow bamboo, in locked chests and boxes and cupboards and bags, deep inside grain stores, buried in the earth, sewn into saris and loin cloths – and of course under the mattress.

7. South Africa does have some MFOs. The best known may be the Small Enterprise Foundation (SEF) but it works in Limpopo province well away from where we carried out the financial diaries.

8. They reached 21 households with loans and a further 9 with savings.

9. The 1999–2000 households were chosen randomly from a group known to be poor; the 2002–05 set from households known to be poor but chosen purposely to get examples of households with accounts at a variety of MFOs, and a few contrasting examples with no MFO account at all.

10 The case of BRAC, Bangladesh's biggest NGO and one of the big-three MFOs in the country, sheds an interesting light on this argument. The groups through which their microfinance work is mainly done have tended to focus ever more narrowly on savings and loans as the years have gone by and the microfinance market has become more competitive. Alongside this, BRAC has developed other more specialized group work for the poor that concentrates on non-financial services but accesses microfinance as a now commonly available resource. See Sulaiman and Matin 2008.

11. This is not to suggest that the poor are any less prone to make mistakes with their financial affairs than other people. It is as easy to find households with very badly managed finances in the slums and villages of developing countries as it is in the suburbs of rich ones.

References

Adams, Dale and Fitchett, Delbert, eds. (1992) *Informal Finance in Low Income Countries,* Westview Press, Boulder, Colorado.

Allen, Hugh and Staehle, Mark (2008) *Village Savings and Loan Associations: A Practical Guide,* Practical Action Publishing, London.

Allianz Bank (2008) 'Do you susu?' [online], available at http://knowledge.allianz.com/en/globalissues/microfinance/alternative_finance/history_moneypool_susu.html [accessed 25 February 2009].

APMAS (undated) 'APMAS' [online], available from http://www.apmas.org/ [accessed 25 February 2009].

Ardener, Shirley (1964) 'The comparative study of Rotating Credit Associations', in *Journal of the Royal Anthropological Institute,* Volume XCIV, London. Reprinted in Ardener and Burman 1995.

Ardener, Shirley and Burman, Sandra, eds. (1995) *Money-Go-Rounds,* Berg, Oxford and Washington DC.

Armendariz de Aghion, Beatriz and Morduch, Jonathan (2005) *The Economics of Microfinance,* MIT Press, Cambridge, Mass.

Arora, Sukhwinder (2008) *Bandhan: Lessons from a New MFI Serving One Million Clients in Six Years,* MicroSave India, Lucknow.

Arora, Sukhwinder and Rutherford, Stuart (1996) *Almirahs Full of Passbooks,* unpublished research report for DFID, Delhi.

Arora, Sukhwinder and Rutherford, Stuart (1997) 'City savers', unpublished research report for DFID, Delhi.

Bouman, Fritz (1979) 'The ROSCA, Financial technology of an informal savings and credit institution in developing countries', in *Savings and Development,* Volume 3.

Bouman, Fritz (1995) 'Rotating and accumulating savings and credit associations: A development perspective', in *World Development,* Volume 23, Number 3.

Bouman, Fritz and Bastiaanssen, R (1992) in Adams and Fitchett 1992.

BusinessWeek (2008) 'Online Extra: Yunus Blasts Compartamos' [online], available from http://www.businessweek.com/magazine/content/07_52/b4064045920958.htm [accessed 25 February 2009].

CDF (undated) 'Sahavikasa: Cooperative Development Foundation' [online], available from http://www.cdf-sahavikasa.net/ [accessed 25 February 2009].

CGAP (undated) 'Ghana' [online], CGAP, World Bank, Washington DC, available from http://www.microfinancegateway.org/ resource_centers/savings/studytour/ghana [accessed 25 February 2009].

Chambers, Robert (1995) *Poverty and Livelihoods: Whose Reality Counts?*, Institute of Development Studies, Sussex University, Brighton, UK.

Charitonenko, Stephanie, Campion, Anita and Fernando, Nimal A (2004) *Commercialization of Microfinance: Perspectives from South and Southeast Asia*, Asian Development Bank (ADB) Manila.

Chowdhury, Farooque, ed (2007) *Micro Credit, Myth Manufactured*, Srabon Prokashani Dhaka.

Churchill, Craig, Hirschland, Madeline and Painter, Judith (2002) *New Directions in Poverty Finance: Village Banking Revisited*, The Seep Network Washington DC.

Christen, Robert (1989) *What Microenterprise Credit Programs Can Learn from the Moneylenders*, Accion International document 4, Washington.

Chronic Poverty Research Centre (2009) *The Chronic Poverty Report 2008–09*, University of Manchester, UK.

Collins, Daryl (2008) 'Debt and household finance: Evidence from the financial diaries', in *Development Southern Africa* 25 (5).

Collins, Daryl (undated) 'The financial diaries' [online], available from www.financialdiaries.com [accessed 25 February 2009].

Collins, Daryl, Morduch, Jonathan, Rutherford, Stuart and Ruthven, Orlanda (2009) *Portfolios of the Poor*, Princeton University Press, Princeton New Jersey.

Developpement International Desjardins (undated) 'Money serving people' [online], available from http://www.did.qc.ca/en/ default.html [accessed 25 February 2009].

Dichter, Thomas and Harper, Malcolm (2007) *What's Wrong with Microfinance?* Practical Action Publishing, London.

Economist (1994) *Pocket Finance*, Economist Books, London.

FAI (2009) 'Financial Access Initiative' [online], available at www.financialaccess.org/ [accessed 25 February 2009].

Forbes (2007) 'The World's Top Microfinance Institutions' [online], available from http://www.forbes.com/2007/12/20/top-philanthropy-microfinance-biz-cz_1220land.html [accessed 25 February 2009].

Grameen Bank (undated, a) 'Grameen Bank at a glance' [online], available from http://www.grameen-info.org/index.

php?option=com_content&task=view&id=26&Itemid=175 [accessed 25 February 2009].

Grameen Bank (undated, b) 'Data and Reports' [online], available from http://www.grameen-info.org/index.php? option=com_c ontent&task=view&id=346&Itemid=416 [accessed 25 February 2009].

Greeley, Martin (1997) 'Poverty and well-being: policies for poverty reduction and the role of credit' in Wood and Sharif (eds.) *Who Needs Credit?*, UPL Dhaka and Zed Books London.

Harper, Malcolm and Arora, Sukhwinder, eds (2005) *Small Customers, Big Market: Commercial Banks in Microfinance*, Practical Action Publishing, London.

Hatch, John (2004) 'A brief primer on FINCA' [online], available from www.haas.berkeley.edu/HaasGlobal/docs/hatch_fincaprimer.doc [accessed 25 February 2009].

Dawkins, Richard (1976) *The Selfish Gene*, Oxford University Press, Oxford and New York.

Helms, Brigit (2006) *Access for All: Building inclusive financial systems*, CGAP, World Bank, Washington DC.

Hollis, A and Sweetman, A (1998) 'Microcredit: what can we learn from the past', in *World Development*, Vol 26 No 105.

Ito, Sanae (2002) 'From rice to prawns: economic transformation and agrarian structure in rural Bangladesh', in *Journal of Peasant Studies*, vol 29, January.

Izumida, Yoichi (1992) 'The Kou in Japan: a precursor of modern finance' in Adams and Fichett (1992).

Jones, Howard (2008) 'Informal finance and rural finance policy in India: historical and contemporary perspectives', in *Contemporary South Asia*, 16(3) September.

McCord, Michael, and Churchill, Craig (2005). *Delta Life, Bangladesh*, Working Paper, CGAP Working Group on Microinsurance. Good and Bad Practices Case Study No. 7, Social Finance Programme, ILO, Geneva.

McGregor, J Allister (1994) *Credit, Debt and Morals: Local and universal models in development practice in South Asia*, based on a paper presented to the European Network of Bangladesh Studies in The Netherlands; unpublished and currently under revision for the University of Bath, UK.

Maxwell, Simon (1999) *The Meaning and Measurement of Poverty*, Overseas Development Institute, London. Available at http://www.odi.org.uk/publications/briefing/pov3.html [accessed 25 February 2009].

Microcredit Summit Campaign (undated) 'The Microcredit Summit Campaign' [online], available from www.microcreditsummit.org [accessed 25 February 2009].

MicroSave (2009) 'MicroSave, Market-led solutions for financial services' [online], available from http://www.microsave.org/ [accessed 25 February 2009].

Montgomery, Richard, Bhattacharya Debapriya, and Hulme, David (1996) 'A study of the federation of thrift and credit co-operatives (SANASA) in Sri Lanka', in Hulme, David and Mosley, Paul, *Finance against Poverty*, (vol 2) Routledge, London.

NABARD (undated) 'National Bank for Agriculture and Rural Development' [online], available from http://www.nabard.org/ [accessed 25 February 2009].

Patole, Meena and Ruthven, Orlanda (2002) 'Metro moneylenders – Microcredit providers for Delhi's poor', in *Small Enterprise Development*, Volume 13 Number 2, June, pp. 36–45, (10).

Platteau, Jean-Paul (1997) 'Mutual insurance as an elusive concept in traditional rural communities', in *Journal of Development Studies*, vol 33, No 6, August.

Prahalad, C K (2006) *Fortune at the Bottom of the Pyramid*, Wharton School Publishing, New Jersey.

Reddy, C S (2008) 'SHGs in India: An interview with C S Reddy' [online], available from www.apmas.org/pdf%5CSHGs%20in%20India.doc [accessed 25 February 2009].

Reille, Xavier and Foster, Sarah (2008) *Foreign Capital Investment in Microfinance: Balancing Social and Financial Returns*, CGAP Focus Note, number 44, World Bank Washington DC.

Robinson, Marguerite (2001 etc) *The Microfinance Revolution, Sustainable finance for the poor*, World Bank, Washington DC.

Rosenberg, Richard (1996) *Microcredit Interest Rates* CGAP Occasional Paper No. 1, CGAP, World Bank, Washington DC. Available from http://www.microfinancegateway.org/content/article/detail/1827 [accessed 25 February 2009].

Rosenberg, Richard (2007) *CGAP Reflections on the Compartamos Initial Public Offering*, CGAP Focus Note 42, CGAP, World Bank, Washington DC. Available from http://www.microfinancegateway.org/content/article/detail/41736 [accessed 25 February 2009].

Rutherford, Stuart (1994) 'CARE and Gher: financing the small fry', unpublished report for CARE Bangladesh, Dhaka.

Rutherford, Stuart (1996) *A Critical Typology of Financial Services for the Poor*, working paper for ActionAid and Oxfam, London and Oxford. Available from http://www.microfinancegateway. org/content/article/detail/1845%20?print=1 [accessed 25 February 2009].

Rutherford, Stuart (1997) 'Informal financial services in Dhaka's slums', in Wood and Sharif (eds.) *Who Needs Credit?*, UPL Dhaka and Zed Books, London.

Rutherford, Stuart (1998) 'The savings of the poor', in *Journal of International Development*, volume 10, number 1, January.

Rutherford, Stuart (2003) 'Money talks: conversations with poor people in Bangladesh about managing money' in *Journal of Microfinance*, Volume 5, Number 2, Winter.

Rutherford, Stuart (2005a) *Grameen II: The first five years*, MicroSave, Nairobi. Available from http://www.microsave.org/ SearchResults.asp?cboKeyword=72&ID=20&cmdSubmit=Sub mit&NumPerPage=10 [accessed 25 February 2009].

Rutherford, Stuart (2005b) *Uses and users of MFI loans in Bangladesh*, MicroSave, Nairobi. Available from http://www.microsave.org/ relateddownloads.asp?id=19&cat_id=289&title=Grameen+II+B riefing+Notes&offset=6 [accessed 25 February 2009].

Rutherford, Stuart (2009a) *The Pledge: ASA, peasant politics and microfinance in the development of Bangladesh*, Oxford University Press, New York.

Rutherford, Stuart (2009b) 'The Poor and Their Money' [online] available from www.thepoorandtheirmoney.com [accessed 25 February 2009].

Rutherford, Stuart (no date) 'Mountain savers', unpublished report for the Central Cordillera Agricultural Programme (CECAP) Banue, Luzon Province, Philippines.

Ruthven, Orlanda and Kumar, Sushil (2002) *Fine-grain Finance: financial choice and strategy among the poor in rural North India*, IDPM 'Finance and Development' Working Paper No.57/2002, University of Manchester.

*Safe*Save (2009) '*Safe*Save' [online] available from www.safesave. org [accessed 25 February 2009].

Schreiner, Mark and Sherraden, Michael (2007) *Can the Poor Save? Saving and asset building in individual development accounts*, Transaction Publishers, New Brunswick (New Jersey) and London.

Sharma, Manohar (2000), *Impact of Microfinance on Poverty Alleviation: What does emerging evidence indicate?*, IFPRI Policy Brief no. 2.

Sinha, Frances (2006) *Self Helps Groups in India, A study of the lights and shades*, CARE, DRS, USAID and GTZ, Delhi.

Sinha, Frances, ed (2009) *Microfinance Self-help Groups in India: Living up to their promise?* Practical Action Publishing, London.

Sulaiman, Munshi and Matin, Imran (2008) 'Making microfinance work for the extreme poor, evidence and experiences from Bangladesh', in *ADB Finance for the Poor, 9*, no. 1, ADB, Manila.

Thaler, Richard (1994) *The Winner's Curse: Paradoxes and anomalies of economic life*. Princeton University Press, Princeton, New Jersey.

Todd, Helen (1996) *Women at the Center*, UPL, Dhaka.

Turner, John F.C. (1972) 'Housing as a verb' in Turner, John F.C. and Fichter, R., *Freedom to Build*, Macmillan, New York.

VSL Associates (undated) 'VSL Associates' [online], available from http://www.vsla.net/ [accessed 25 February 2009].

Vogel, Robert 1984, 'Savings Mobilization: the forgotten half of rural finance' in Adams and von Pischke, *Undermining Rural Development with Cheap Credit*, Westview Press, Boulder, Colorado.

Vander Meer, Paul, Mu-shan Hung and Slusser, William (2009) 'Rotating Savings and Credit Associations and the Economic Takeoff of Chulin Village, Taiwan' Department of Geography, California State University, Fresno, USA.

Von Pischke, J D (1991) *Finance at the Frontier*, World Bank, Washington DC.

Wikipedia (undated) 'Credit Union' [online], available from http://en.wikipedia.org/wiki/Credit_union [accessed 25 February 2009].

WOCCU (2008) 'World Council of Credit Unions' [online], available from http://www.woccu.org/ [accessed 25 February 2009].

World Bank (undated, a)' Understanding poverty' [online], World Bank, Washington DC, available from: http://web.worldbank.org//WBSITE/EXTERNAL/TOPICS/EXTPOVERTY/0,,content MDK:20153855~menuPK:373757~pagePK:148956~piPK:216 618~theSitePK:336992,00.html [accessed 25 February 2009].

World Bank (undated, b) *INDIA Self-help Groups, Savings Mobilization and Access to Finance* unpublished study.

Wright, Graham A N, and Mutesasira, Leonard (2002) *The Relative Risks to the Savings of Poor People*, MicroSave, Briefing Note # 6, Kampala. Available from http://www.microsave.org/SearchResults.asp?cboKeyword=18&ID=20&cmdSubmit =Submit&NumPerPage=10 [accessed 25 February 2009].

Yaron, Jacob (1994) 'What makes rural finance institutions successful?' in *World Bank Journal*, World Bank, Washington DC.

Yunus, Muhammad (1982) *Grameen Bank Project in Bangladesh: a poverty focussed rural development programme*, Grameen Bank, Dhaka.

Yunus, Muhammad (2002) *Grameen Bank II : Designed to Open New Possibilities*, Grameen Bank, Dhaka.

Yunus, Muhammad (2008) Creating a World Without Poverty – Social Business and the Future of Capitalism, PublicAffairs.

Index